FASHION JEWELRY TO MAKE YOURSELF

RENATE BOSSHART

FASHION JEWELRY TO MAKE YOURSELF
IMAGINATIVE, REFINED, ELEGANT
WITH INSTRUCTIONS

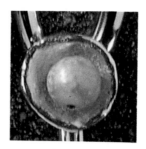

PHOTOS - ULRIKE SCHNEIDERS
TEXT - SABINE FELS
DRAWINGS - ANNA SALUZ

Schiffer Publishing Ltd

77 Lower Valley Road, Atglen, PA 19310

Photos on pages 2 and 3:
See instructions of pages 30 and 106.

ISBN: 0-88740-874-5

This title was originally published under the
title *Modischer Schmuck zum Selbermachen*
by Georg D.W. Callwey GmbH & Co., München.

Printed in the United States of America

Library of Congress Cataloging-in-Publication Data

Bosshart, Renate.
    Fashion jewelry to make yourself: imaginitive,
refined, elegant, with instructions/Renate
Bosshart; photos, Ulrike Schneiders; text, Sabine
Fels; drawings, Anna Saluz.
        p.   cm. -- (A Schiffer craft book)
    ISBN 0-88740-874-5 (pbk.)
    1. Jewelry making. I. Fels, Sabine. II. Title
    III. Series.
    TT212.B67 1995
    745.594'2--dc20   95-34075
                                CIP

Published by Schiffer Publishing, Ltd.
77 Lower Valley Road
Atglen, PA 19310
Please write for a free catalog.
This book may be purchased from the publisher.
Please include $2.95 postage.
Try your bookstore first.

We are interested in hearing from authors
with book ideas on related subjects.

CONTENTS

FOREWORD

Fashion has become an important component of our daily life. Whether casual spare-time clothes or formal evening wear, we express our personality and our moods with our choice of clothing. Fashion makes countless suggestions to us, but it does not obligate us to follow one single line. We have the freedom of choice—relaxed or strict, extravagant or simple, and the favorite pieces that we like to wear give us a good feeling of harmony and security. And jewelry is a part of what we wear. It is completion and emphasis, and as varied as fashion itself.

The desire to decorate oneself ranks among the basic human needs. Individuality is expressed in decoration; preferences and styles are reflected in it. The origin may be sought in cultural religious rites, but very early in history, jewelry served primarily to mark the individual person. Pieces of jewelry defined the social rank of the male or female wearer, gave information about the wearer's wealth and family standing, and heightened the splendor of special festivals. One attributed magic powers to them, wore them as talismans or protective amulets, and used them as a source of wealth and means of payment.

For a long time, all of this has stepped into the background. Jewelry for the women of today is first of all the perfect completion to the fashionable outfit, the "dot on the i" for a carefully assembled wardrobe, the sparkling focus of formal evening attire. It is not restrained elegance, but rather eye-catching individuality, that matters most.

What is more important than discovering one's own creativity and combining the truly unique from the multitude of beads? Have you not stood in a jewelry store, full of ideas and scarcely restrainable joy, trying to choose from the pieces of jewelry to find one that is just right for you? Never has the choice included as much as today. The spectrum extends from the simple artificial pearl to the piece of Murano glass, from wooden imitations to costly gilded components, and only a few basic techniques are needed to create individual pieces of jewelry out of these treasures.

In this book you will find over a hundred examples with thorough instructions, and you will see that much which appears to be complicated is based upon one simple idea and can be copied easily, even by a beginner. It is best to begin with the introductory chapter, which will acquaint you with the materials, basic techniques and tools. And then just let inspiration come to you! You can copy the models—in the appendix you will find a long list of sources—or be moved to make your very own creations. Put in a small supply of nice beads, wires and clasps, and then you can turn spontaneous ideas into reality immediately and give your wardrobe that certain something, even at the last minute. I wish you much joy in discovering and creating.

Renate Bosshart, Zürich

WORK AND MATERIALS

WORKPLACE

The most important prerequisite for a suitable workplace is good light. Natural light is most suitable, because it is necessary for color determination. Lay out your work surface so that tools and materials are within easy reach, and so that you can lay out the piece of jewelry on a flat surface. Many creations should be viewed at a little distance to see their effect; for this, a not overly small mirror is useful, with the help of which you can also determine the final length of a strand.

MATERIALS

Whatever pleases you is allowed—and the possibilities are infinite. Once you have found pleasure in individual and unique jewelry, you will discover that components of fashion jewelry are offered in an incredible variety. Let their richness inspire you, but choose with care, for cheap products that lose their beauty in just a short time are not worth the trouble.

Beads should be filled, especially when you intend to thread them. The most beautiful and expensive beads are made by hand in the Murano region of Italy. Every bead is unique and gives a piece of jewelry an aura of uniqueness. But the variety of simpler glass beads is also fascinating: matte or glossy, smooth or decorated, in delicate pastel tones or slightly changing—you will have a hard time deciding.

Plastic components will be found in every imaginable shape. They can be combined imaginatively with beads and have the advantage of being light. For brooches and earrings in particular, this is an important factor.

When you obtain gold-plated components, make sure you get a good quality. Merely etched pieces quickly lose their gloss and make your work worthless.

Ceramic components with beautiful glazes give a rustic, powerful effect, and can be used effectively as individual pieces, with little else added, to form striking strands. Make sure their surfaces are not too rough.

A special mention is deserved by *aqua-leather*, which has only been rediscovered in the most modern times. It is tanned fish skin, particularly that of salmon, which resembles snakeskin optically but is much less problematic in terms of protecting species. The leather is very durable and can be worked very well.

If you belong to the ever-growing ranks of people with allergies, then the word *nickel* will surely sound an alarm for you. The manufacturers of fashion jewelry and its components have reacted to this problem and are working hard to make substantially nickel-free products, unfortunately at the cost of the components' brilliance. Good and also optically pleasing results can be attained through the use of a new type of palladium base: jewelry components that are on the market as "nickel-allergy-free" are prepared in a palladium bath that is allowed to contain only a small amount of nickel. To avoid allergic reactions, look for the appropriate labels.

CHOICE AND DESIGN

Jewelry is a matter of personality and type, and before you decide to create or duplicate a model, you should be clear as to what style suits you: are you a silver or a gold type? Does a long filigree or a short compact strand go better with your hair style and stature? Which colors dominate in your wardrobe? Do you prefer simple elegance, or do you love eye-catching effects? In this book you will find inspirations for all types, which you can develop creatively through your personal choices of colors and selection of individual components. If you prefer to duplicate a model precisely, you will find a list of sources in the appendix.

The introductory chapter gives you an overview of the basic techniques that form a basis for all models and involve varying degrees of difficulty. To develop a feeling for the interplay of various elements of jewelry, threaded strands are a good place to start: If an initial composition does not please you, you can do the piece over without great difficulty. If you have found a strand that you especially like, begin by reading the instructions for making it, and look carefully at the illustration, so as to get an impression of the degree of difficulty involved. Strands that look very simple often require a great deal of experience, because every process must be done just right. By following the step-by-step photographs, it will be easy for you to learn the basic techniques quickly, and you will find out how fast you develop the necessary nimbleness of finger.

TOOLS AND EQUIPMENT

PLIERS

Good pliers are the most important tools in your jewelry workshop. To start with, you should have pliers to press press-molded beads together (upper left) and side-cutting or rosary pliers (upper right). Very useful for neat work on snap clasps are the handmade pliers with varying hole sizes (below); they are, alas, not cheap, but you can work very precisely with them. One alternative is a pair of pliers with three different holes, though this is less precise.

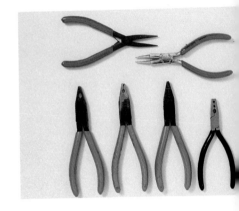

LEATHER BANDS

Leather bands come in various thicknesses and many colors, either by the meter or in one-meter pieces. They look very attractive in combination with rustic ceramic components. Notice that dark bands easily become prone to breakage and lose their color if they are knotted or penetrated too often.

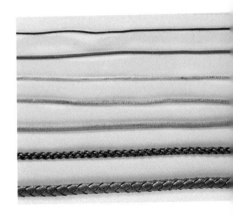

CORDS

Gloss or matte, smooth or rough cords made of cotton or viscose material can be found in the notions department of a department store as well as in the arts-and-crafts department. They can be matched easily to the colors of your clothing and your choice of beads, and look just right with a cord clasp (see pp. 13ff). If you want a more casual effect, knot the cord lightly and let the ends hang down loose.

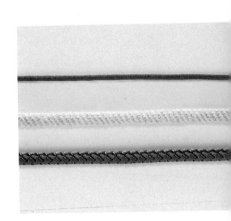

PVC BANDS

PVC bands are remarkably durable; they can be knotted, inserted, and reused again and again. The transparent band is especially suitable for threading transparent glass or plastic beads, while a black band should be chosen above all when it will help define the piece of jewelry and be visible between the strung beads. You will make the threading easier if you first run a knife or scissors lightly along the PVC band and let it slide through your hand several times, so that it warms up and thus becomes thinner and more flexible.

This technique is especially useful for strands on which the beads are set loosely, so that the band remains visible. In time, heavy beads will stretch the PVC band and it may become necessary to rework the clasp.

WIRES AND THREADS

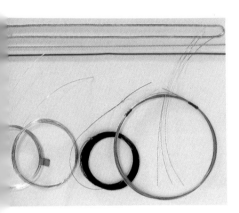

For all the models in the book, you will find a precise listing of the carrying material used. Among your materials there should be the following wires and threads in various thicknesses:
Left: Silver- and gold-plated wire with a copper base.

Right: Black nylon thread.
Far right: Nylon thread.
The choice of a thickness is dependent upon the diameter of the smallest beads.
Top: A finished chain made of aluminum.
Below: Thin aluminum tubes.

CLASP CAPS AND RINGS

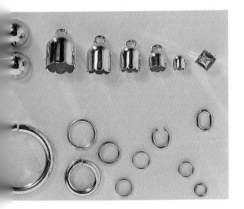

Top: Clasp caps with and without eyelets, in various thicknesses, for use as caps or threading components. Four thin tubes, such as are used in some models, fit precisely into the square cap on the right.
Below: Rings with various diameters and different thicknesses. When working with them, make sure to close the rings cleanly, so as to avoid damaging your wardrobe.

The thin rings can be closed with pliers, while for the heavier ones you should use two pliers, which requires a bit of practice.

PINS AND PRESS-MOLDED BEADS

Press-molded beads and end-crimps or "callottes" (above) are very necessary equipment, of which you should lay in a not too small supply. Separating components of gilded metal (right) are available in various sizes; they can be used in many ways, often with an amazing effect. Also needed in the basic supplies of your workshop are pins, with and without eyelets, in various lengths and head sizes (below).

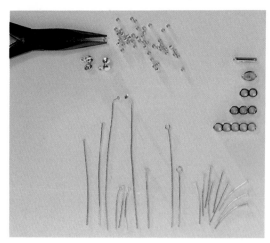

EAR CLIPS

Do you like to wear earrings? Then an assortment of ear clips and piercings should not be missing from your supplies. The choice ranges from simple ear pins through half-creoles and creoles in many different sizes to clips with flat front plates, to which you can attach decorative components.

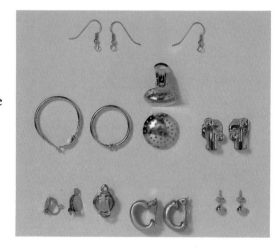

SPECIAL TOUCHES AND REFINEMENTS

Small items often make the work easier. Here is a choice of special elements with which you can achieve astounding effects:

Upper left: Into the ring with a thorn, which can be hooked easily into a half-creole, you can glue a pearl or something similar. Cloth or leather bands, for example, can be attached to the teeth of the next ring. The next item is always needed to make a hole smaller to prevent small beads or thin tubes from sliding into the considerably larger orifices of larger beads while stringing.

Center: The overbuttons can have a bead or other decorative element glued onto them and be fitted over a blouse button. Through the round disc with two rear tubes, you can thread nylon wire, and then glue your creations onto the front of the disc. In some models, a small tube with small holes on both sides is used. This takes a bit of skill to fit a wire through, but the effect is astounding.

Below: Three brooch pins with attachment surfaces of different sizes.

TECHNIQUES

THREADING

Threading is the simplest and quickest technique for making a strand. Let the models or whichever beads please you particularly inspire you to make your own creations and try them to see what fits together. You will soon notice that unusual combinations can have a very lively and interesting effect. Glass beads can be combined wonderfully with gilded or silvered components, while large and small beads often harmonize very well too. When combining them, consider also the weight of the material, for an excessively heavy strand is not pleasant to wear. If you want to save material, work the strand from the middle toward the back and concentrate the nicer components in the front area. For the back of the neck, you can choose simple beads or lengthen the clasp with a few spring rings.

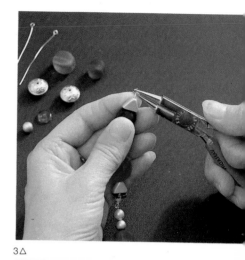

3△

1△

2▽

PINNING

Pinning ranks among the basic techniques of jewelry production and can be used in a great variety of ways. Pinned strands have a less compact effect and are simultaneously more mobile than threaded ones, but on the other hand, they demand more patient preparation.

On an eyelet pin (available in various lengths) you can thread one or more components. The rest of the pin, if it is too long, can be shortened with the side-cutting pliers to about one centimeter and shaped into a small eyelet, which does not need to be closed completely. The eyelet is made most easily if you turn your hand toward the outside (2) and bend the pin toward you (3). Then insert a new pin in the eyelet (4) and close it carefully (5). Proceed in the same manner until the strand reaches the desired length.

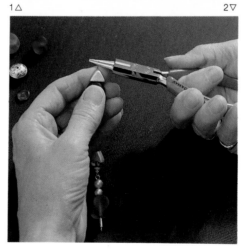

4△

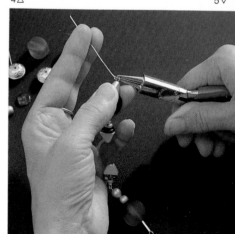

5▽

MAKING SPIRALS

For some models, spirals of gold or silver wire form the focus of attraction. They are available as double spirals, which you can separate easily: Separate the spiral in the center until it breaks into two parts, which you can work separately.

TWISTING

Some models are made with twisted nylon filament, on which you can thread small beads. To do this, draw a piece of filament about 55 centimeters long over the metal part of pliers or scissors. Leave a piece straight at each end to make threading easier.

1△   2▽   3△

PIERCING A CORD

Would you like to take a combination threaded on nylon filament and attach it to a cord? A little trick helps you to do this: Stick a thin metal tube through the cord (1), through which it is easy to thread the nylon filament (2). Now you can remove the tube, put a bead on, and secure the composition with a press-molded bead (3). The excess can be capped with the side-cutting pliers.

2△

STITCHING METAL NETS

Metal nets can be had in a variety of sizes and shapes. Cut yourself a piece of wire about 60 centimeters long, with a thickness of about 0.4 mm (or substitute thin nylon thread), and secure it to the net by twisting the short end around several times (1). Now push the wire from below through the hole of your choice, put a bead on it, and push the wire back through to the underside. Pull the wire tight, hold it in place with your fingertip, and push it through to the front again (2). In this way, one pearl at a time, you can decorate the whole net. Any first doubts about success disappear with the progress of the work; the more artistically you work, the more the results will please you.

CLASPS

A nicely made clasp is much more than just the practical aspect of a piece of jewelry, and does not need to be hidden. Even when it is not essential in technical terms—for instance, on long strands—it looks professional and finishes your piece of jewelry. So don't avoid the work that a carefully made clasp requires, and make a careful choice from among the numerous possibilities. The models in this book offer you a richness of inspiration as to shape, and you should make the choice on the basis of the style of the strand. Here is a selection of clasps and accessories of which you should have a small supply on hand (see photo on the right):

Top: Various sizes of hook clasps. Keep a supply on hand, for only a hook clasp

suited in strength to the piece of jewelry will hold reliably and be workable.

Above: Two gilded decorative clasps for fancy strands.

Left center: Twist clasps in different shapes; they look very professional and can also be worn in visible positions.

Right center: Swivel hooks in various shapes and sizes. With the big ring in the center, you can double a long strand or combine several thin strands into an impressive piece.

Below: Various ring clasps and one decorative ring-staff clasp, which will complete many luxurious strands ideally.

The schematic drawings on the next pages will make clear the techniques of making the most important clasps.

Clasp for 2 to 5 mm PVC bands, also for leather bands

With a 5 mm clasp, you can hold up to five leather bands. To do that, you may need to separate the clasp with two pairs of pliers.

Clasp for 1.2 mm PVC band

For a very thin band, the smallest clasp is still too large, so double the band and cut off the excess.

Simple Ring-Bar Clasp

Pull the PVC or leather band through the eyes of the clasp and push the clamps down, after having removed the eyes from them. A clamp can be closed most evenly with hole pliers, but it can also be done with flat pliers as long as you work carefully.

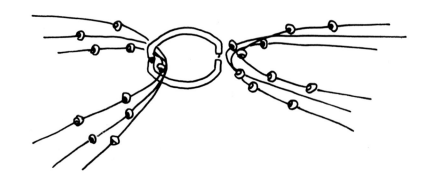

Snap Clasp

With a snap clasp you can shorten a strand. Fold the strand on itself to the desired length, twist it a little, and link the ends with a snap clasp, which can be opened again at any time.

Ring-Bar Clasp for a Cord

First bind the cord strongly with thread and put an eyed clasp over it. A strong ring binds the caps with their own clasps.

Classic Cord Clasp

You stick the cord fast with tape before the unraveled end (1) and trim it back somewhat (2). Put a drop of glue in each of the two clasp caps, let it dry somewhat, and press the glued cord ends firmly into the caps (3). Make sure in advance that the band of tape is completely concealed.

1△   2▽   3△

Bundle Clasp

Up to 24 leather bands may be bundled. To do this, wrap the bands firmly with thread, tie it tight, and trim the ends to the same length. Try various cap sizes to see which one fits most precisely, put some glue on the outside bands, and push the cap on firmly. A small ring links the caps with the swivel hook.

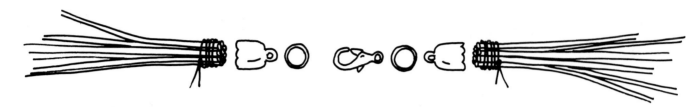

Twist Clasp

This clasp is best suited for thin nylon wire or nylon thread, which you can pass through the eye of the clasp and secure with a press-molded bead. The thread and clasp eye can also be linked with a small ring.

If you are working with several strands, then join the individual eyes on a small intermediate ring.

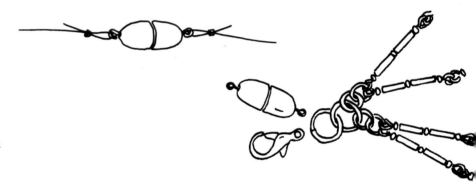

Clasp with a Press-Molded Bead

If you have used nylon filament or nylon thread for threading, and the length of the strand is definite, add on a small eyelet with the help of a press-molded bead. Attach the clasp of your choice to the eyelet.

Clasp with Press-molded Beads and a "Concealer"

Additional types of clasps are shown on pages 32, 59, 61, 82, 110 and 114.

THE MODELS:

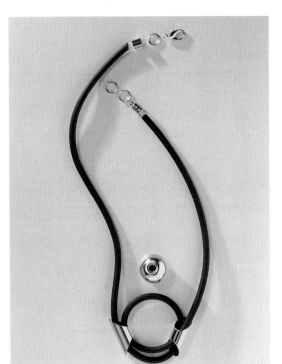

ZIP ZAP

ZIP ZAP 1 + 2

Time is of the essence, and you still haven't found the right piece in your jewelry box? Try creating a new piece, quickly made out of a few individual parts. You need a dark cord or a black PVC band (5 mm thick), two gilded tubes cut at an angle, and perhaps a thick bead with a wide opening. Now put the band through the tubes, attach a clasp (how to do that is shown in detail in the "Clasps" Chapter), and—zip zap!—you are finished.

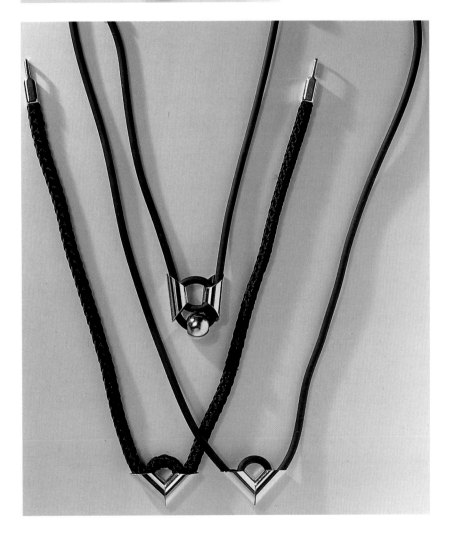

For the strand on the left, make each of the three pendants out of two gilded tubes and two times three beads, which you thread alternately on transparent PVC bands. The knot, which is meant to hold them firmly in place, so that all the components are linked stiffly without any play, is best concealed in one of the three tubes. Push all three components onto a loop in the dark PVC band (5 mm thickness), which you have put through two diagonally cut tubes (see Zip Zap 1). Make the clasp with a push-snap fastener, split rings and swivel hook, as described in the "Clasps" Chapter.

A single pendant, as in the model in the center, can also be made very simply, linking two long tubes of gilded metal by threading the center bead of the group of three between the two beads of the necklace.

The strand on the right was threaded and can be worn easily without a clasp.

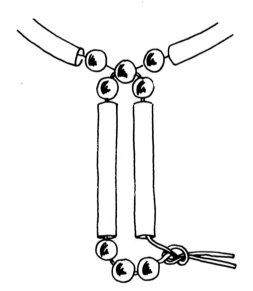

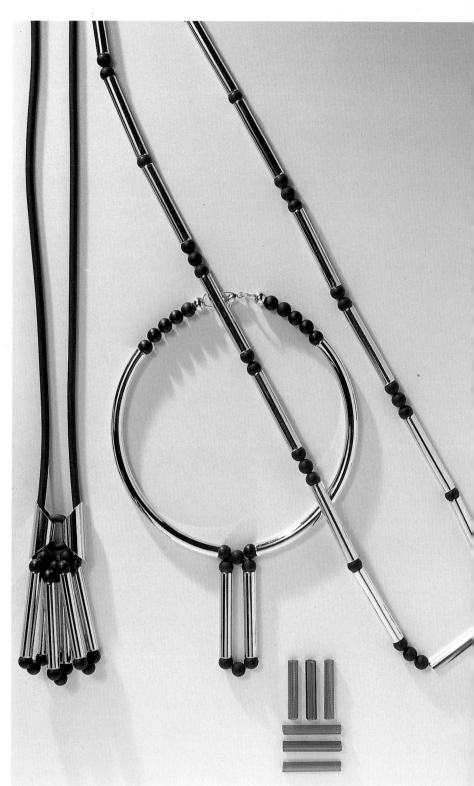

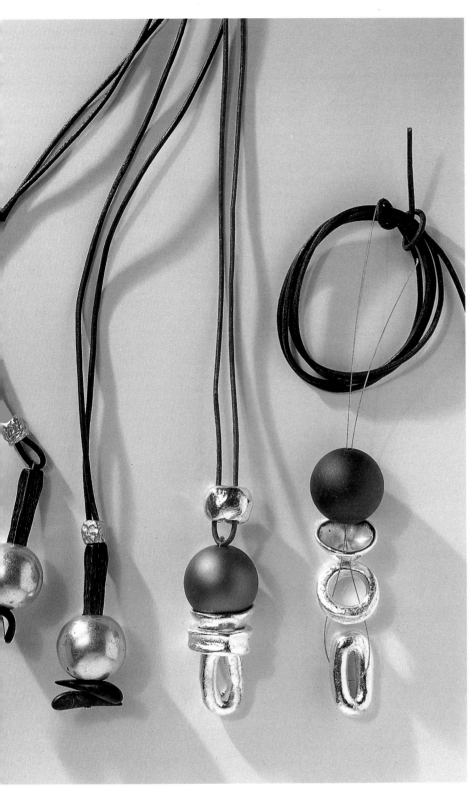

This attractive pendant on a leather band can be made quickly out of left-overs. For the pendant on the left, you need a particularly long nail-like pin, onto which you place the components according to the model or your own conceptions. Bend the excess into a small eyelet, through which you thread a suitable leather band. For the finishing of the eye, slide a bead with a particularly large hole over both bands. To finish it, knot the bands or install a simple clasp.

For the pendant on the right, thread a silver-plated ceramic component on a nylon thread, bring the ends together, and slide the other components on. Finally, attach the leather band and secure your composition with a press-molded bead. Trim off the excess thread. Here too, a wide bead or a broad ring completes the attachment point.

The elephant in the middle can be placed on the strand very simply. The gold spiral fits right over the eyelet, through which you have already run a leather band. The pendants on the left and right vary the theme of pinning (see Zip Zap 4) and should be fun to try and combine, test and evaluate. You will certainly have the best ideas.

A few leftover wooden beads from your last vacation—in no particular order—threaded on a leather band and closed with an original bead-knot, look just great.

These small discs of ceramic come in many colorful glazes, with a very nice, lively surface. They can be used in a helter-skelter fashion, or, as here, in groups of contrasting colors. To make the threaded discs stay completely even, choose a band—PVC is most suitable— that fills the holes in the discs as completely as possible.

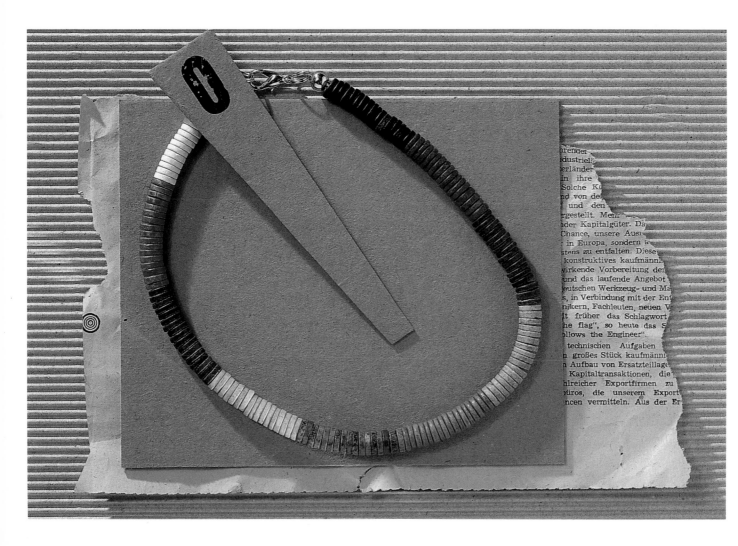

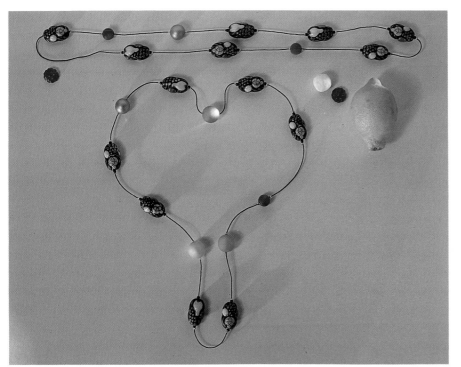

ZIP ZAP 8

This strand looks good enough to eat: Hand-painted beads, colorful and juicy as a bowl of fruit. Just thread these original bits of fruit onto two black nylon threads (length of the model: 1 meter) and put single-colored beads in bright summer colors between them. The strands can be made without clasps; just push the ends through a bead crossways and put a press-molded bead on either side. Trim off the excess. The strands have the most eye-catching effect when you wear both of them; they can turn any simple T-shirt into a summer star.

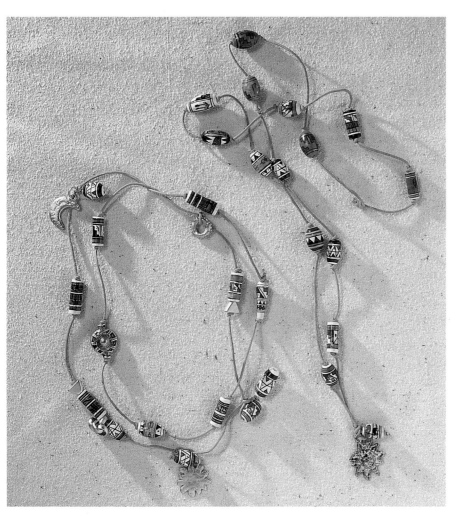

ZIP ZAP 9

Do you still have a handful of beautiful beads that you bought at a colorful bazaar under the southern sun? Then simply put your vacation memories on a chain. Use one or two leather bands, which you can knot together in very rustic fashion, and put on colorful beads that you can hold in place with two side knots. If that is too commercial for you, then string a few little golden bits between them to relax the mood.

ZIP ZAP 10

To make these brooches, look for long hatpins with nice end pieces. The two brooches in the center have the pin firmly attached to the cone, while the end pieces on the right and left are gilded or silvered. Fill the pins as full as you can. Flat rings, small beads, or short pieces of aluminum tubing are useful and decorative bits with which you can fill the pins tightly, without spaces, so that there is even room for the end piece (which can be secured with a drop of glue). On the back of a large, flat piece—in the upper third of the pin, if possible—you can glue a suitable brooch pin.

ZIP ZAP 11

These varied cone pendants can be made with a built-in eyelet or, as in these four examples, with a glued-on pin. For these pins there are end pieces in gold or silver, but you can just as well glue on a nice bead. Choose materials according to your own imagination, but make sure that the pin is really filled up. About halfway up, work a cord in. For the pendant at far right, push an 8 cm pin through a slightly bent metal tube, form a small eyelet, and thread this decorative element on.

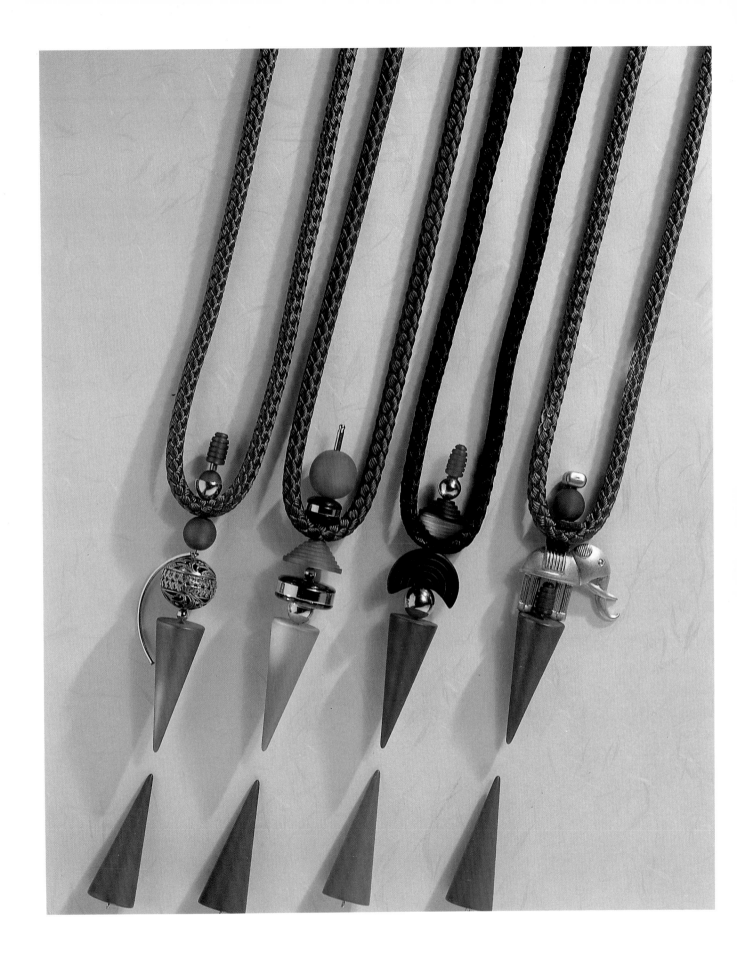

ZIP ZAP 12

These are actually stick-pins to which decorative beads and cords have been added in very original fashion. To fill the pin so snugly, you have to do a bit of testing and perhaps put a small bead or slim ring between the other things.

To close them off, use simple metal end pieces, which can be purchased along with the pins. For the clasp, don't be satisfied with a simple knot, but use a cord clasp or a push-snap fastener.

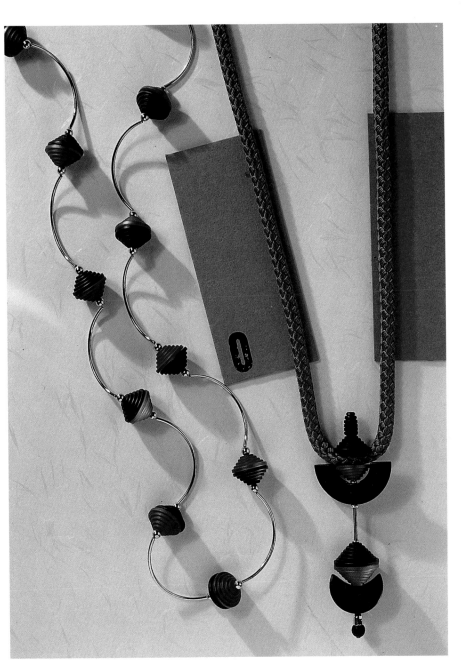

ZIP ZAP 13

For the long strand on the left, you need about a meter of nylon thread for stringing. Small beads prevent the thin tubes from sliding into the holes of the bigger beads.

The shapes and colors of the pendant contrast nicely with each other. The carrier of the composition, the center of which is stressed by a small piece of aluminum tubing, is again a very simple stick-pin. If you want to be absolutely sure that nothing can come loose, then secure the pin closing with a drop of glue.

Plastic cones in harmonious proportions are eminently suitable and can be combined with many shapes and materials. All the pendants have been made by the same principle. Run a 15 cm nylon filament through the eyelet of the cone and thread whatever beads you choose onto the doubled wire as you wish. The combination looks especially complete if you can conceal the small cone eyelet in a cap or a bead with a large hole. Finally, form an eyelet with a press-molded bead and hang the piece on a leather or cotton band or a necklace. To use as earrings, use a small ring to link the cone with the earring itself in half-creole form. The result is very simple and down to earth, yet very elegant.

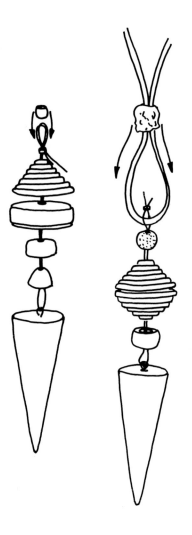

BEACH

BEACH 1

The bright shimmer of a sandy
beach in the warm sunshine and the
blue of the sky and sea set the tone of
these simple, bright pieces.

Impressions of summer: sea shells, sand and sun, plus three strands that steal the show from any T-shirt. A nicely wound cord and summer accessories are the main ingredients of them. For the strand at lower left, wrap the ends of a cord 1.2 meters long firmly in transparent tape and cut them diagonally. Now you can easily thread six gilded tubes and five thick beads alternatingly. When you have threaded and placed all the components, trim off the taped ends and push the ends of the cord into one of the tubes, into which you have first put a drop of glue: finished! Wear the strand long or shortened, the latter with a snap clasp.

For the pendant in the middle, unite four nylon wires about 15 cm long with a press-molded bead and push a small bead over the gathered wires. Thread the components on according to the illustration (for the part made of two small tubes, separate the wires). Now lead two wires at a time around the cord, bring them together again, and add a press-molded bead. Small and larger beads cover the attachment. They are fixed in place with press-molded beads. To emphasize the center, put on two wide metal tubes. It looks very original if, instead of using a cord clasp, you glue the ends into two metal caps (use a strong glue) and decorate them with small ornaments. The strand can be knotted at the back of the neck.

The separate pendant of the strand on the right is made from top to bottom. Push a particularly nice and not too small bead onto a band of PVC about 30 cm long (thickness 1.2 mm), bring the ends together, and thread on the slightly curved, gilded ceramic disc from the arched inside surface. With three firm knots, unite the decorative elements and the center of the cord. With the two ends of the PVC band, work downward separately. First thread on a separating element, two thin metal tubes and a second separating element, before you push the two ends together through the nice ball that sets the tone of the closing. If you like your arrangement, tie a double knot as close to the bead as possible and cut off the excess. In one last work process, place two metal tubes over the cotton band, one from each side, and press the ends into two cord clasps already prepared with glue.

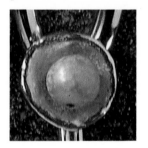

BEACH 3

The plastic beads of these two optically impressive strands are like a collection of seashore treasures. They come alive completely in the harmony of the individual elements and leave a lot of room for your imagination. From the richness of materials, choose what pleases you and lay it all out before you start to work. Each strand has a final length of 60 cm, so you need about 1.20 meters of material. The strand on the left was threaded onto nylon wire and closed with a ring-and-rod clasp, the strand on the right was pinned and made without a clasp (for techniques,

BEACH 4

The principle used in making this unusual piece of jewelry is not difficult, though it does require your sensitive fingertips to combine and unite the components harmoniously. First pin the components, about fifty of them at first—for the most part, small pieces of coral were used—onto pins. Lay out a chain of large links, about 50 cm long, and tie a PVC band (thickness 1.2 mm), likewise 50 cm long, onto the far end. Now thread the band through the links of the chain and push some three or four of the pinned components per link onto it. To lighten the impression, always put a bead between them, and make the strand more lavish toward the middle. The big starfish will also mark the middle of the strand. It is best to put the strand on to check the layout and determine the right length. The simple swivel clasp can be done according to the illustration.

BEACH 5

Are you looking for a strand that is quick and easy to make and yet has an extremely refined and unique effect? Here it is. The gentle contrast of matte pearly-white and gold components gives this strand its exclusive character and makes it look especially beautiful when worn with a simple piece of clothing. For a length of about 45 cm, you need eleven galvanically gilded double spirals, which you cut apart. Straighten the outer end and then slide the bead on. By using pliers, pull the gold wire through until you can stick it back in the other end (you need a good hearty pull). A drop of glue secures the bead in case the tension of the wire is not sufficient. Put the individual spirals side by side and link them with small rings as the combinations please you. An unobtrusive swivel hook closes this original strand, for which you should select beautiful and impressive pearl beads.

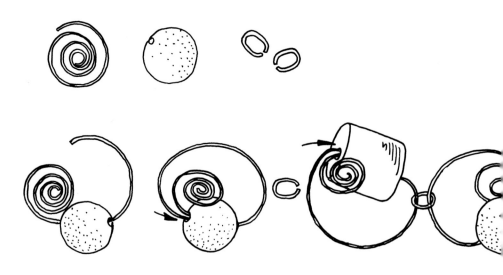

BEACH 6

These two strands are as light and bright as a beautiful day at the beach. For the model on the right, cut two lengths of nylon filament about 50 cm long. Form groups of large and small decorative elements as you wish, and hold each in place with a press-molded bead on each side. Include one or two beads in every group, to create a more easygoing overall impression. The clasp—here a ring-bar type—can be made as explained on page 14.

The long strand on the left has an even, calm feel to it. On three one-meter strands of transparent PVC filament (1.2 mm thick), string one, two, or three matte pearl beads, held 1.5 cm apart by two press-molded beads each. Several larger components, such as fish or shells, lighten up the mood. The three strands are held together by a push-snap fastener clasp and closed with a swivel hook.

BEACH 7

Do you still lack a bright, sprightly summer accent for your ears? These merry earrings are easy to make. Assemble them as shown in the drawing.

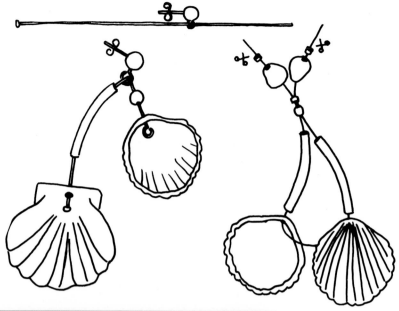

BEACH 8

This very unconventional knotted strand that will excite your imagination and inspire it to create its own designs. The combination of golden and matte white parts gives this piece of jewelry its light effect. First, string the elements of your choice on pins and bend the ends into eyelets, to which you attach small rings. After you have decided on the groupings and divisions, thread the elements onto the natural-color leather band, 3 mm thick and 1 to 1.20 meters long, and attach them with a simple knot. Alternating pins and individual pearl beads create a particularly nice effect. A simple knot, or, if you want to make it a little more elegant, a swivel hook or screw clasp will finish off the strand.

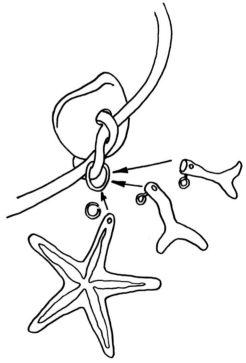

BEACH 9

Sea shells, amphorae, fish, and even a little frog decorate this strand of matte-white elements and many small beads. To complete it, follow the directions for the Glass Bead Game 11 model.

BEACH 10

These short necklaces are examples of how different effects can be achieved with practically the same elements. The principle involved in making the two outside strands is the same. First select a curved, gilded tube, through which you pass a transparent PVC band 4 to 5 mm thick; the thickness depends on the diameter of the tube, which should fit snugly around the PVC band. Through the eyelet of the cone you thread a piece of nylon filament some 20-30 cm long. Pass the ends of the filament through the first beads and then separate them and pass them around the side of the tube. Hole reducers harmonize the transition between beads of different sizes. Above the tube, bring the filament ends together again before you thread on the last beads. A small press-molded bead forms the closing. Pull the nylon filament as tight as possible, using pliers, so that the upper beads don't come loose. Make the clasp any way you want.

The center strand is made in similar fashion, but you are working with two nylon filaments, which you thread through the beads together. Four small, bent tubes form the closing here, which in turn is secured with a press-molded bead. Sling two suitably colored leather straps around the tubes and select a clasp.

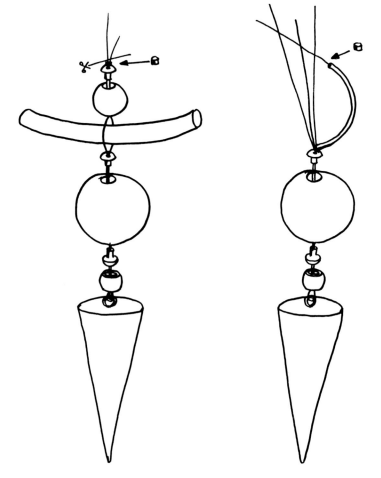

AFRICA

AFRICA 1

Wonderful accessories in glittering gold plate, beads in dark natural shades, and rustic cords give these pieces of jewelry in African style their emphatic character.

AFRICA 2

This simple strand takes up the theme in a technically simple but very effective manner. It is threaded on a nylon filament about one meter long. An eyelet forms its starting point; you push the filament through a small press-molded bead, make a loop and put the filament back through. With flat pliers, squeeze the press-molded bead together. Now you can add beads and tubes as you wish. The strand has a more interesting appearance if you vary the basic scheme slightly—here dark and golden beads are bent in alternation with tubes in semicircular form. When the strand reaches the length you want, cut off the filament to about 1.5 cm and again make a loop. The strand is closed with a screw clasp which you can fasten to the loop with a small ring.

AFRICA 3

For this necklace you need a little patience, in return for which you will enrich your jewelry box with a really impressive piece in African style. And it is much simpler to make than it appears. The nucleus of it is formed by a natural leather band, 2.5 to 3 cm thick, with a length of about 55 cm. In the first work process, you pin gold and imitation wooden beads to make units two to five centimeters long, bend the excess into an eyelet, and string them on a natural leather band, some 20 cm long and 1 mm thick. The more often you begin with a gold component, the more brilliant the ultimate effect of the necklace will be. In the second step, attach these elements, starting from the middle, to the carrying band with a simple knot (see the drawing). Push a single bead over the thin ends of the band, and secure it to the leather band with a tight knot. The more elements you attach, the thicker the necklace appears to be. For a nice effect, make sure that the center element is especially lavish and make it a little longer. The closings at the two ends are formed by a few simple beads with wide openings, which you slide over the thicker leather band. Attach a twist clasp as in the photo, or alternatively a swivel hook, as in the drawing.

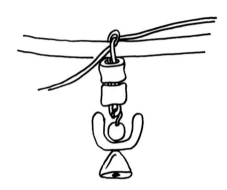

Two summer strands, as if created to catch the eye on a simple dress or T-shirt, can be made in no time flat. The strand on the left is threaded, and thus appears heavier and more compact. Its special charm is its alternation of gloss and matte elements. The more the darker components vary, the more harmonious the golden sections will appear. Components of different lengths also heighten the exciting effect of the strand, which is closed by two rings and a twist clasp.

The strand at the right is pinned and has a lighter, more mobile effect. Do not choose too many different elements of imitation wood, gold and ivory. Put those you select on eyelet pins as you wish. Accept as a ground rule that the bigger and more compact the individual elements are, the fewer beads belong on the pin. The strand comes to life because of the variation of similar elements. It can be closed with a clasp of your choice, or if it is long enough, it can be made without a clasp.

AFRICA 5

For this pair of earrings in an African style, make two short chains of thick and thin elements. Thread the bottom link onto a nylon filament 30 cm long, with small wooden beads and curved tubes, which you bend into a circle. Pass the ends of the filament towards each other through the uppermost link and then together through the gilded beads and caps and the large imitation-wood plastic beads. At the top, make a loop of the two ends of the filament, and close it with a press-molded bead (finish it off with a large-holed bead). Fasten the pendant to the ear clip with a small ring.

AFRICA 6

It will not be easy for you to make a choice from the wealth of beautiful, galvanically gilded decorative elements. For this optically heavy chain, which looks particularly decorative on a dark background, stylized, flat elephants, stars and a crescent moon with a patterned surface were chosen. Select a screw clasp that matches the thickness of the chain links and does not interrupt the smooth flow of the chain.

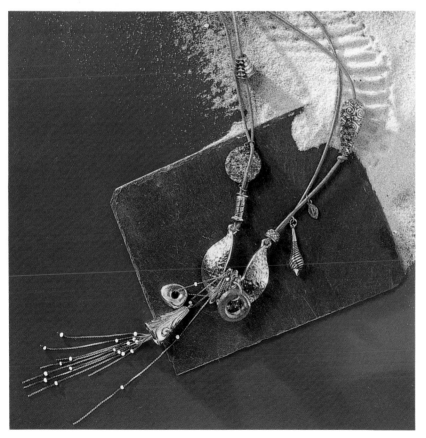

AFRICA 7

If at some time you have no brilliant idea for a strand, then let some beautiful components inspire you. You will be surprised at what can result. The simple ground rule: select a particularly striking component as the optical center and work in smaller elements to both sides. The midpoint of this strand is a large U-shaped unit, through the eyelets of which thin leather bands have been drawn. Delicate chains, bunched, knotted, and set with small beads, accent the center. Attach the smaller components to the leather bands with eyelets, knots or a drop of glue, at whatever place they look best. The effect will astound you.

This colorful, lively strand can be made very simply—provided you make sure that all the materials go together properly. Above all, the hole diameters of all the beads, of which you will use many in varying sizes and colors, should be the same, and should fit snugly onto the black PVC band. Cut the bands (3 mm thick) one meter long and slide the small ceramic discs onto them. If you hold the band under flowing hot water and draw it through your hands several times, it will become slicker and somewhat thinner. To finish it, attach a 5 mm push snap fastener clasp and a swivel hook.

The striking, washed-out stone is not a purchased component, but still has its own particular charm by including such a vacation souvenir in the strand.

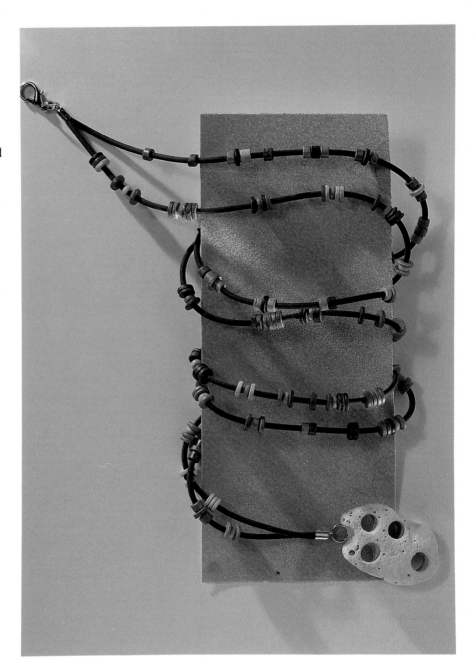

Take any quantity of Rocaille beads, as many strands as you please, about 85 cm long, of a thin, strong nylon thread, and whatever nice individual beads or leftovers suit you, and this happy strand is finished and ready to liven up any overly simple piece of clothing. Using a small press-molded bead, form a small eyelet at the beginning of each strand, and then go to it: Thread several Rocaille beads on and bravely put larger beads among them. It is really surprising how different colors, shapes, and materials will harmonize when combined with each other. The nicest effect is gained from an unobtrusive twist clasp, which you can attach as shown on page 16.

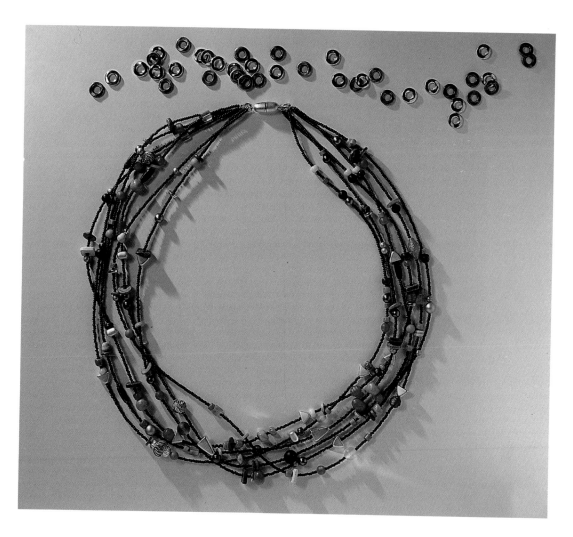

AFRICA 10

Leather bands, now available in many bright colors, go ideally with ceramic components. As a rule, ceramic beads have a large opening, which allows you to put a doubled leather band through them. First knot the band in the middle, double the ends, and thread the beads on. For the strand at the left, first thread the large ring onto a piece of nylon filament, then put the silvery ball and the big blue bead onto the doubled ends. Use the filament ends and a press-molded bead to form an eyelet, which must be just wide enough to thread the leather band through. To finish off the union, thread the smaller, silver-glazed bead over the doubled leather band. If the colors harmonize, several such strands look very good when worn together.

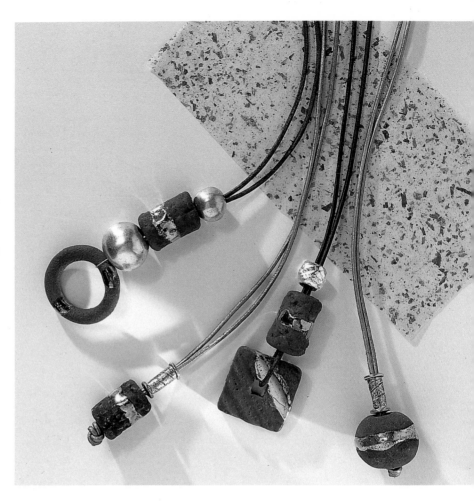

AFRICA 11

As much, as colorful, as dense as possible—that's how to make this striking strand out of colorful ceramic components and black PVC band, the latter as thin as possible. To hold every disc, knot the band, which is about 90 cm long, once and push the bead right onto the knot. A little caution and feeling are called for when you do this! After dividing a dozen discs evenly along the strand, knot the ends of the band and trim off the excess. If you want, make one strand with small gold beads to lighten up the effect.

This short necklace has been created based upon the pattern of opulent African jewelry and looks positively amazing on tanned skin. Cut six strands of 1.2 mm thick PVC band, each about 60 cm long, and thread alternating long bone beads and small dark discs onto them. Begin and end with a dark bead, and always thread two strands through a hole in the leather dividing element. Bring the strands together through a large bead, and hold them with a 5 mm push-snap fastener clasp. The piece is finished with a swivel hook. It looks especially nice when you twist the strands a bit before putting it on.

A matching belt completes the African look. The carrier material is transparent PVC band, onto which, in steady rhythm, light and dark bone beads, glass beads and gilded plastic beads are threaded. Dividing elements of thick leather, which you can either buy ready to use or cut to size yourself, can be applied at regular intervals to hold the bands in position.

For the earring on the right, cut a natural leather band 1 mm thick and 15 cm long and make an eyelet in the middle; tie it off with wire. Now hang the big flat ring on, pass the bands through a bead, and make a good-looking knot. When you hang the eyelet on a half-creole earring, the job is finished. For the earring on the left, unite two perforated ceramic discs with two thin metal tubes, through which a piece of PVC band is passed and then tied backward. Glue an ear clip on the back of the upper disc. These two earrings are so eye-catching that they make a particularly good impression when worn alone.

Ceramic and leather go together very well, as shown here in this short necklace. For the carrier material, select a natural-colored leather band, 4 to 5 mm thick. As shown in the drawing, sling 20-30 cm leather bands (2 mm thick) around the thicker band and then tie the hanging elements on. The ceramic discs tied close to the carrier band conceal the bands beneath them. Ceramic components are made more irregular than glass or plastic pearls, and some holes will be too big for the leather knots. You can easily remedy this by placing smaller beads or, as in the model, irregularly shaped metal pieces in front of the big holes. When you have tied all the elements in place—the central piece measures about 20 cm— you can still do a little sliding and arranging until you really like the results. Fill in each side with a few beads, but leave a piece of the leather band visible so the strand won't become too heavy-looking. If you include a few additional spring rings by the clasp, you can vary the length of the strand. Make the clasp as shown on page 13.

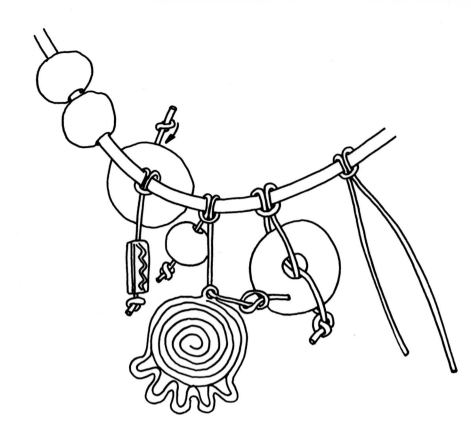

HARMONY OF COLORS

HARMONY OF COLORS 1

Nice colors, perhaps determined by your wardrobe, and five evenly matched strands or beads are very important for the effect of this necklace. Choose transparent PVC band matching the holes in the beads, and first decide on the length of the inside strand, which should circle your neck closely. The necklace gains added sturdiness and lies more flat thanks to six dividing elements, which you place in the middle, on both sides, and at the closing. Now thread the beads on according to the illustration. Find out by how many beads the individual strands have to be enlarged from the inside outward, and make sure that the dividing elements have the same position on each side, so they'll be exactly opposite of each other. The work involved in counting the beads exactly will be rewarded in the even circle of the piece. Secure the ends of the PVC bands with push-snap fastener clasps, attaching a small ring to each of them. Now attach these small rings to the clasp with one big ring.

HARMONY OF COLORS 2

Disc upon disc, ring upon ring, and this colorful strand is finished. It's child's play.

HARMONY OF COLORS 3

Do you like this strand? Then don't be appalled by mere numbers. About 700 little discs and just as many small rings must be strung if you want to wrap five strings of beads decoratively around your neck. With a bit of practice, the work can be done fairly fast—really! Make sure to get the soft rings that can be opened easily. To do that, hold the pliers with the ring in your left hand and open with the right hand: open the ring, put on the beads, close the ring, hook the next open ring on, put on the beads, close the ring...Five strands, each in a solid color, full of contrast or matching, any way you want them. For the end pieces, pin a triangle and a thin tube and put the small colored discs on. You can wear this piece around your neck like a kerchief and entwine the strands once.

HARMONY OF COLORS 4

For this pair of earrings, combine small metal and plastic rings into five strands each, all of differing lengths (the metal rings can be bent easily with pliers). Look into your supplies for a long pin with as big of a plate as possible, and thread the short strands onto it. Then put the pin through the cap, star, and decorative cage ball, and form an eyelet. With a small ring, the pendant can be fastened to an ear clip or ear hook.

HARMONY OF COLORS 5

Long pins are the secret ingredient of all these earrings made of nice glass elements. Follow the detailed drawings or find your own inspiration for your unique creations.

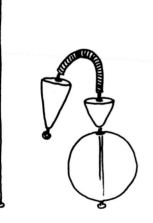

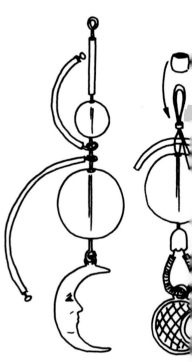

Gleaming glass drops in golden
settings, combined in a glittering chain
for a woman who loves vivid colors. The
drops, in three sizes and many shades of
color, can be attached to each other
with rings or pieces of chain. The work
doesn't take long, and the effect is
classic and costly.

Like a dream from childhood days: Two strands of glass beads, colorful as candies. And it's not only children who will have a taste for them. String the discs and beads on black PVC band, and hold the arrangement on with press-molded beads. Very simple and very merry—jewelry for good-mood days, simply knotted at the end.

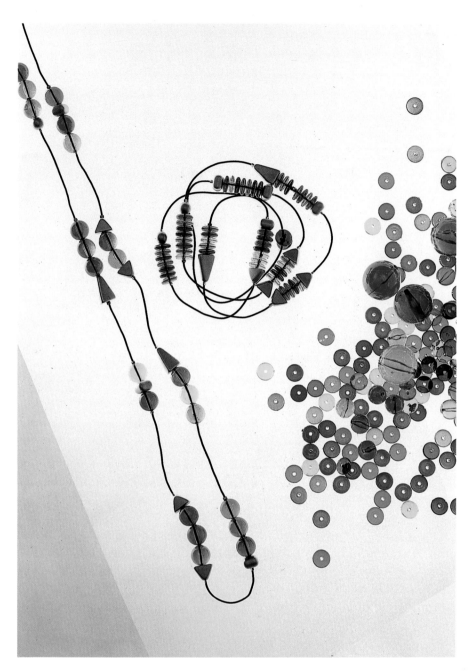

The hanging pendants of glass that really shine and sparkle look simply terrific on this rather wild chain. Attach the pendants with small rings between the long gilded tubes. To make the five threaded strands of different lengths, thread different numbers of gilded beads on the ends. Make the clasp as shown in the drawing.

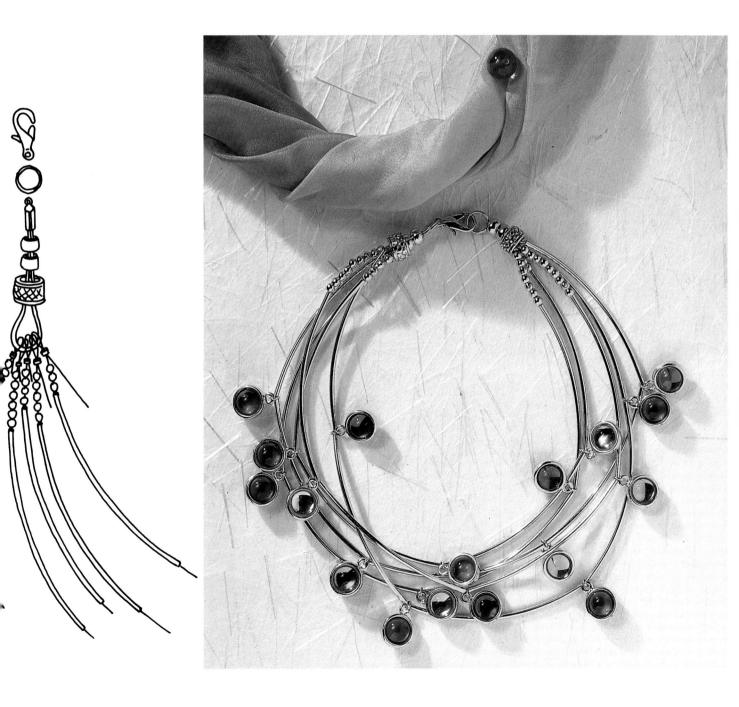

The example in this photo is shown doubled, but is meant to be worn alone, with its arrow-shooting little Cupid pendant. And that's the way you put it on the strand: In the first step, pin seven caps with seven colorful discs onto pins and close each with an eyelet. For this model, seven different colors were selected, but it also looks good in a single color. Through the small eyelet on the figure, thread a 1.2 mm PVC band, double it, and thread the other elements on. If the arrangement looks good, shorten the PVC band, pull it somewhat stiff, and put a push-snap fastener clasp on it that finishes it off with a large-holed bead. A split ring, gilded tubes, and two cotton cords complete the strand.

You can make the earrings according to the drawing, using a holed plate that you fasten to the appropriate ear clip.

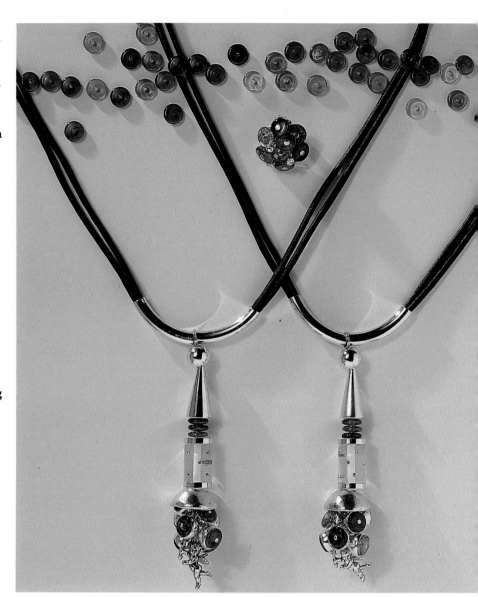

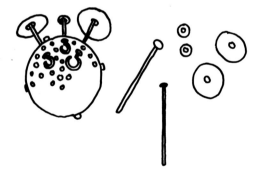

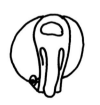

HARMONY OF COLORS 10

Twenty-eight triangles in four colors are combined to make a snugly packed necklace. Thread these unusually shaped beads onto two nylon filaments, each 50 cm long, as shown in the drawing below. If you now make the inner filament somewhat tighter, the impressive round shape will take form. Two beads and a large tube finish off each end of the strand.

HARMONY OF COLORS 11

Do you like colors and enjoy a clever piece of jewelry? The colors of the rainbow provided the inspiration for these strands of flat plastic beads. The beads for the strand on the left are threaded onto a dark PVC band, the thickness of which should be matched to the hole's diameter so that the beads cannot slide, even without knots and glue. For the pendant, pull a black nylon thread about 10 cm long through the ring of the little plastic shoe, pass both ends through the big bead and the flat discs, and fasten this unit to the strand with an eyelet and a press-molded bead. For the strand on the right, prepare a transparent PVC band on which, following either the illustration or your own preference, you string the flat discs. If you like symmetry, then work from the center out and make the fields of color exactly equal. The two pendants can be made on pins with eyelets and fastened between the beads by using small rings. The two small teddy bears are also hung from the eyelets by small rings.

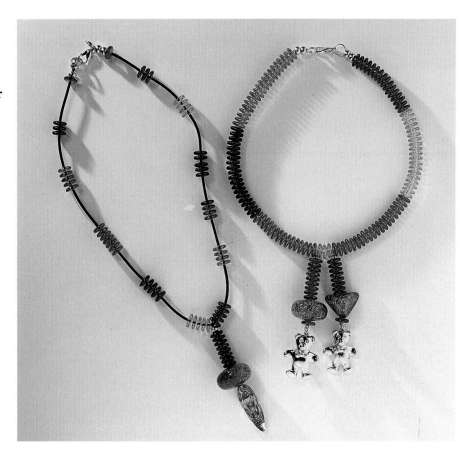

HARMONY OF COLORS 12

Technically, this strand is absolutely not a problem; the beads are threaded onto a nylon filament and the strand is closed with a twist clasp. All you need are eye-catching beads and harmonious connecting pieces, which should be very unobtrusive in order to emphasize the effect of the beautiful beads of Murano glass. When you put the mixture together cleverly, even simpler beads can look very good alongside of the more expensive Italian glass beads.

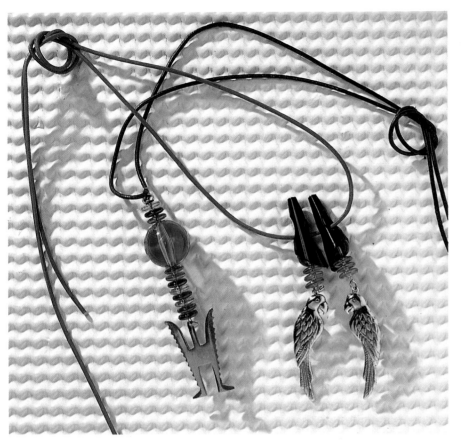

HARMONY OF COLORS 13

Do you have a few nice beads left over, as well as a pendant that you especially like? With a little imagination, you can conjure up a new piece of jewelry very quickly. Either thread the elements onto nylon filament as shown on the left, or string the individual pieces onto a long pin with an eyelet, as with the pair of birds on the right. You can also feel free to liberate an older piece of jewelry from its solitary existence in a dark corner of your jewelry box and give it new life by using a new and different arrangement.

HARMONY OF COLORS 14

The earring in the middle, with the nice decorative elements, is worked from top to bottom. Through a small piece of aluminum tubing you slide two pieces of black nylon thread, each about 20 cm long, make a sling and thread the small cap, the fantastic ball and the crescent moon over all four ends. Secure them with a press-molded bead, and apply another to the four threads, which you have first cut to different lengths, to hold small decorative pieces. The result is a lovely, unique piece that you can hang on a matte-silver half-creole clip.

The two outside earrings are assembled from bottom to top, beginning with the stylized birds, which you can thread onto nylon filament. The ends are passed together through the other beads, and a small sling with a press-molded bead forms the closing.

There are 1001 possibilities for making a unique piece of jewelry in no time out of small bits and pieces. Such five-minute earrings are small gifts with a flair. On the eyelet of a not overly long pin, hang a teddy bear or clown or whatever. Push the bead onto the pin, bend the excess into an eyelet, and use a small ring to attach the result to an ear clip or pin. And it's finished!

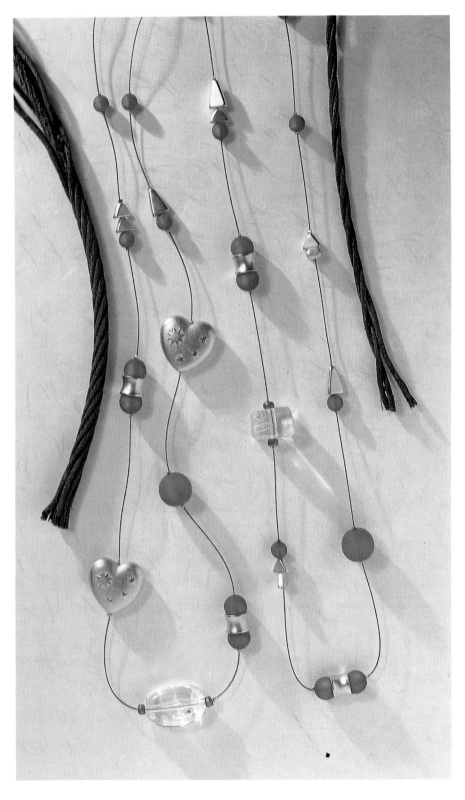

THREADS AND ROWS 1

These strands, for which it is very important to select the right combination of components, look as weightless as filigree. Try a few possibilities and check the total effect before you attach the individual groups to the nylon thread with small press-molded beads. There are also colored cords on the market, and you can match the beads with them, but the carrier band should not be too colorful because the thin line has an important effect on the impression made by the strand. You can make these strands, which are 70 cm long as illustrated, without a clasp at all. Just push the two ends of the cord through a big bead, one from each side, and put a press-molded bead on either side, over both cords, to secure them. On the other hand, you can achieve a more complete effect with a delicate twist clasp. The two strands can be worn one over the other.

THREADS AND ROWS 2

When you want to mix small, simple
beads with big, fancy beads, the strand
has a lighter look if you place decorative
metal tubes on both sides of the larger
elements. The little gold beads prevent
the tubes from disappearing into the
holes of the larger beads. A very elegant
and amazingly simple solution to the
problem. For the clasp, see page 16.

THREADS AND ROWS 3

Striking individual pieces often
provide the inspiration for a whole
strand, as the nice stylized elephant
does here. Brown and silver give this
object, threaded onto a nylon filament,
a very harmonious and not overly
contrasting effect. To save material, short
chains were added in the back-of-the-
neck region. But you should make sure
that this simple material cannot be seen
on the sides, where it can disturb the
whole effect of the strand.

GLASS BEAD GAMES

GLASS BEAD GAME 1

The same elements can be combined in ways that are eternally new and remarkably different. This pendant features striking metal tubes in an unusual combination. Begin with two nylon filaments, each about 20 cm long, and place a press-molded bead on one end of each. Now thread them on separately as far as the orange glass bead, and from there together to the small golden triangle. The bent tube should be placed about in the middle. Try it until the composition looks balanced. Finally, put a press-molded bead on both filaments and trim off the excess. The green glass bead, set on a doubled nylon filament, makes the connection with the gilded necklace, which can be worn neatly around the neck.

GLASS BEAD GAME 2

Make this strand with two nylon filaments, which you separate for the tubes. You can vary the system by replacing one of the two parallel tubes with a row of small beads.

Two earrings in different color combinations. One all in shades of one color, the other with strong color contrasts. Both of them are simple to make, and thus exactly right for you if you are still relatively inexperienced. Cut a nylon filament, about 20 cm long, for each earring, and then thread the U-shaped element on. Then thread them separately through the wooden plate and the two tubes, and finally bring the threads back together through the gilded cap and the big glass bead. With the help of a press-molded bead, form a small eyelet, which you can cover with a large-holed bead, and trim off the excess thread. Now all you need is a suitable ear clip to hang your composition on—and an effective piece of jewelry, which you can also wear very well as an individual piece, is finished.

The black pendant shown below also looks complicated without being it. You place all the elements onto a particularly long pin, the end of which you shorten, if necessary, and bend into a small eyelet. The only difficulty is in the decorative spiral of silver wire. Partly untwist a half spiral a little bit and insert it in the two holes of the silver tube. It will look very nice in contrast with the black grooved disc. If you like, you can also glue a decorative, fanciful bead onto it.

GLASS BEAD GAME 4

For the pendant on the left you need two curved glass tubes and three nice beads of Murano glass. On each of two nylon threads, about 10 cm long, you thread three curved tubes of glass and metal. In a second step, you fasten the tube ends together, push one of the two irregular beads on, and set a press-molded bead. With a 15 cm nylon thread you attach both units by leading the thread around a metal piece and sliding the glass bead, metal tube and metal bead over the united thread ends. Pull them tight and fasten with a press-molded bead. Through the holes in the sides of the gilded metal tubes, pull a leather band.

A thin, bent metal tube is the special ingredient of the pendant on the right. Cut two pieces of nylon thread about 10 cm long and unite them with a press-molded bead. Cap the excess. The four green glass rods are threaded onto separate filaments, and for the other elements, attach the ends together. Attach the curved metal tube firmly between the two filaments. Form an eyelet and set a press-molded bead, but not before you have first pulled the threads tight again. The metal tube pushed onto them must now stay firmly in place and not be able to slide off. If it doesn't work out quite right, a drop of glue will help. A softly falling aluminum ring looks especially nice with this pendant.

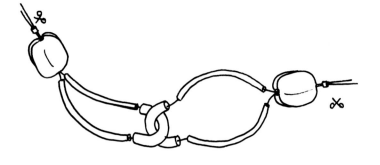

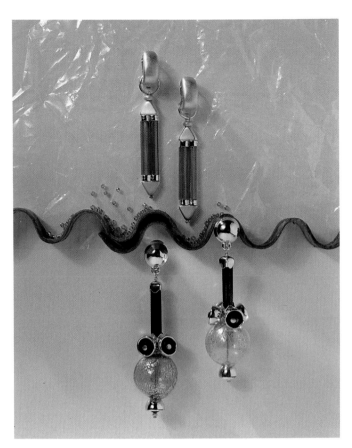

GLASS BEAD GAME 5

You can make the green earrings with two pieces of nylon filament, about 10 cm long, that you link with a press-molded bead. The two triangular beads are threaded onto the pieces of filament while they are attached together; then they are separated to take the other elements. Finally, form an eyelet with the help of a press-molded bead, cover it with a small bead, and hang as small a loop as possible in a golden ring, which hangs in a half-creole.

The earrings at the bottom of the picture are made according to the same principle, but here you unite five filaments with a press-molded bead, so you can thread the five thin black glass rods on individually. The small caps with black beads are attached separately and threaded on after the large Murano glass bead.

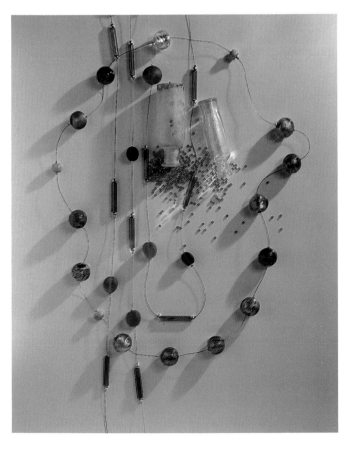

GLASS BEAD GAME 6

Beads made of Murano glass are so radiant that they look noble even, and especially, in simple settings.

First determine the length of the strand and the positioning of the beads. Every element is held in its position on the nylon thread by two press-molded beads, and you can easily vary the distances of the beads from each other a little. The loose sequence actually emphasizes the uniqueness of the expensive beads. All three strands were made without a clasp. Simply push the thread ends crosswise through a big bead and secure each end with a press-molded bead. The strands can be worn either long or doubled.

GLASS BEAD GAME 7

A lively trio on a black cord, created from an unusual idea and a handful of leftover Murano beads. For each of the three elements, link four 15 cm nylon threads by using a press-molded bead. Thread the entire bundle through a gilded metal bead, a colorful glass bead and a four-cornered cap. Now the paths of the four threads diverge for the central piece made of four times two rods and a pearl, before you bring the bundle back together again. After adding the second colorful bead, pull the threads tight, and hold them in place with a press-molded bead. Shorten the threads to various lengths and thread three Murano beads and one glass heart onto each, securing them with a press-molded bead. On a thick black cord, the three little crowns look very jolly and very unconventional.

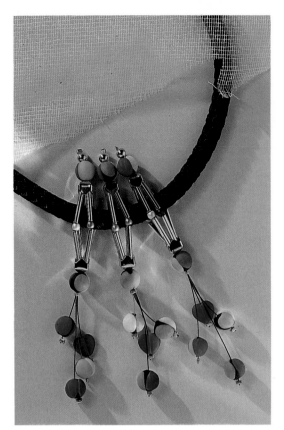

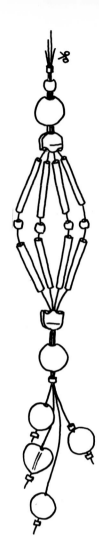

GLASS BEAD GAME 8

A snugly fitting necklace of beads and rods, this will surely catch every eye. Beginning with one small bead, thread three beads and two black glass rods 3 cm long onto a pin about 8 cm long. Bend the end into an eyelet. After you have thus secured the individual elements, bend the rods in the middle, making various angles. Thread these elements, alternating with small beads, onto a PVC band. When you have come up with your correct length, secure the ends with a push-snap fastener clasp, which can be finished using a large bead with a wide hole, and fastened onto a ring with a swivel hook as the clasp.

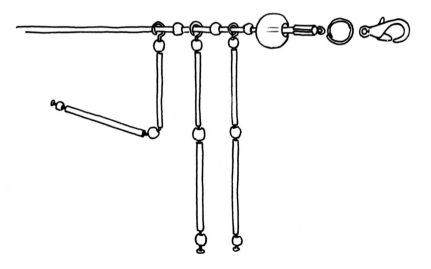

Mouth-blown Murano glass beads undoubtedly rank among the most beautiful of all beads. Whoever has been able to watch as they are produced one by one in Venice—every bead unique in size and structure—will value them particularly and also understand why their price is high. For this short necklace you will combine eight large green beads with genuine gold inlay and small pinned bead grapes into a costly piece of jewelry. The glass balls are hollow inside; therefore the relatively stiff nylon filament is recommended as the carrier material. In case you have only the softer nylon thread on hand, you can push a thin tube through each bead in order to make threading easier. To make the grapes, thread groups of nine pinned caps (pin, bead, and gold cap) between the large beads.

The closing is formed by five caps on each side and a clasp as shown in the drawing on page 14.

GLASS BEAD GAME 10

Twenty-two of these lively curved glass tubes are threaded onto each 50 cm nylon filament. Always place glittering gold elements and large glass beads between the tubes. To begin and end the three strands, make small eyelets, and slide them onto a PVC band (thickness 1.2 mm) about 6 cm long. Now thread a small gold wheel and two beads onto each of the gathered band ends. After the second large bead, attach a 2 mm push-snap fastener clasp, concealed by two small large-holed beads. Such a clasp, made somewhat longer, saves expensive material and also lies on the neck very well. Clasps are not merely functional parts, but also play a large role in the impression made by a piece of jewelry.

GLASS BEAD GAME 11

A low-necked dress is the proper frame for these strands of small glass beads. Both are made according to the same principle and, strictly speaking, consist of two strands about 45 cm long, held together by a strong ring and closed with a ring-rod clasp. Thread the glass beads on according to the drawing here, and hang small gold metal parts or hearts pushed onto metal pins on the side eyelets.

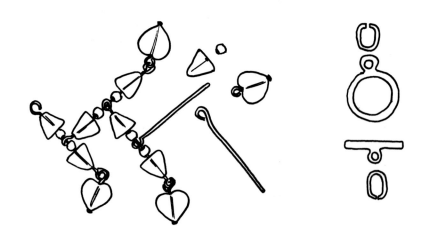

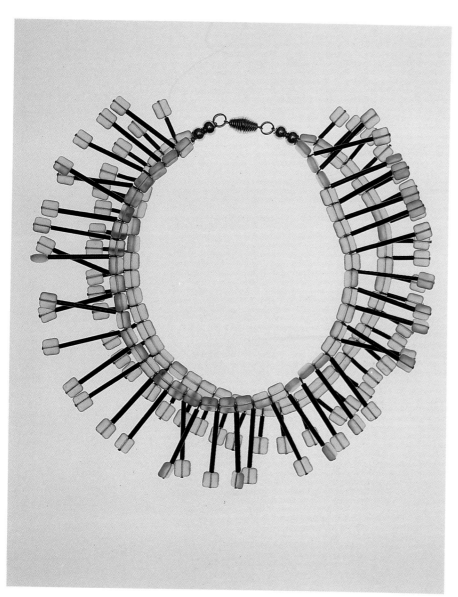

GLASS BEAD GAME 12

Rhapsody in Blue—a blue dream for blue hours, made of wonderful matte glass beads that were designed according to old patterns. The carrier material is nylon filament, two pieces cut to 45 cm length. In the first work process, place 37 long and 41 short pin and bead elements on pins which you bend into small eyelets above. Beginning with one bead, thread alternating pinned elements and beads onto both strands and secure the ends with small eyelets. Fasten the two strands together—the strand with more elements goes above— and push large-holed beads over the eyelets and press-molded bead. Two split rings, or more to lengthen the strand, and a twist clasp finish the blue necklace.

GLASS BEAD GAME 13

These beautiful glass beads in delicate tints were made new from patterns at the Gablonz Glass World and used here to make a particularly elegant and expensive summer necklace. You need about 200 glass beads in different colors, which you will slide onto pins and secure with bent eyelets. To give the chain a somewhat looser effect, combine a quarter of all the beads with a thin glass rod. Thread them on a PVC band 1.2 mm thick and about 60 cm long, and double the last centimeter of the end and push it into a 2 mm push snap fastener (see page 14). Fasten the clasp firmly with hole pliers and hang a spring ring on the eyelet, fastening a swivel hook to it. If you want to conceal the push snap fastener clasp, slide a metal bead with a large opening over it before you start the threading. Thread the pinned beads on in groups of four or five, arranging them so that the longer elements are distributed evenly over the entire strand. To keep the necklace from becoming too compact or using too much material, use glass beads threaded directly onto the carrier band to separate the individual groups. Determine the length of the strand according to your neck size and secure the end with a push snap fastener, metal bead and eyelet. You can lengthen the strand by adding several spring rings, hooked one to another.

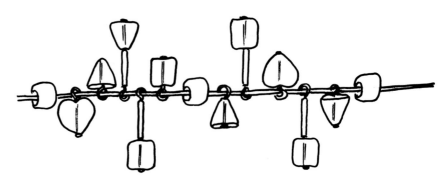

THE RIGHT TWIST

THE RIGHT TWIST 1

Rocaille beads, galvanized discs and press-molded beads are the materials for this strikingly long strand that is assembled out of approximately 75 individual rings. On a black nylon thread 15 cm long, thread about 30 rocaille beads and one small golden disc. Put the ends of the threads crosswise through a press-molded bead and close it firmly. The ring length should be selected so that part of the thread remains visible and the beads have a little play. The outer excess thread can be capped as near to the press-molded bead as possible. Thread beads onto the next thread and pass it through the previously finished ring before you close it, and thread the disc of the previous ring onto it. One piece at a time, the main strand takes shape, consisting of about thirty rings.

The model shown here also gains in effect from 45 additional rings which are threaded without discs and pulled through two adjoining rings before being closed.

Wear the strand either long and without a clasp or as a short necklace, closed with a cap clasp.

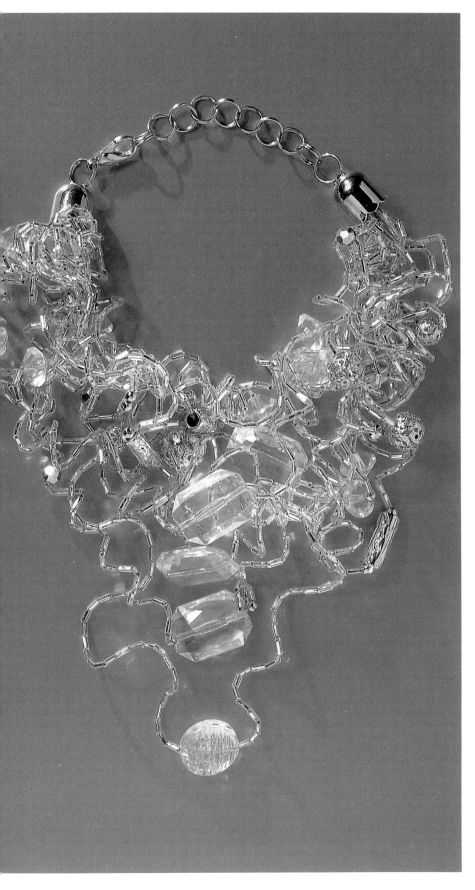

THE RIGHT TWIST 2 + 3

Would you like a playful atmosphere instead of having everything strictly in straight lines? Certainly there will be something in your wardrobe that is suitable for this kooky strand and the one on page 82. Although they look very complicated, they are astonishingly easy to create. And once you have figured out their secret, you need only a little imagination when you choose the beads. The solution to this puzzle is a nylon filament drawn over the metal piece of a pair of pliers, making it behave like gift-wrap string after twisting: it forms waves. The greater the tension, the smaller and tighter the waves become. For threading, leave one end straight while making an eyelet in the other.

For the strand on this page, prepare ten nylon filaments 50 to 60 cm long and thread silver glass rods onto them. Large transparent beads and golden filigree beads form attractive contrasts. The gray of the rods and the reflecting silver beads threaded between them make the necklace on page 82 look cool and a bit technological. If you prepare the eight strands with less tension, the waves remain more open.

Close the strands with a second eyelet and fit a clasp according to the directions on page 82.

THE RIGHT TWIST 3

A variation on Model 2: Black and white rods, threaded alternatingly onto thirteen strands and accented by transparent and black beads, liven up this lavish and yet light necklace, which is made with the same twisting technique. The clasps of both pieces can be made according to the drawing.

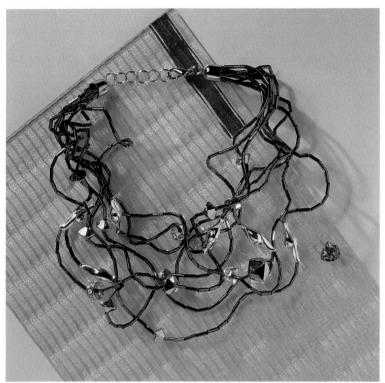

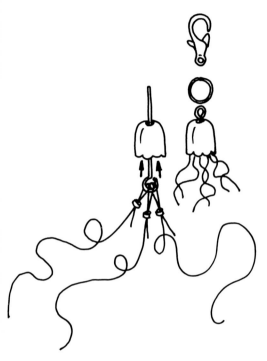

THE RIGHT TWIST 4

Little beads and thin rods can be combined with each other very nicely. You can thread the two types of elements alternatingly on nylon filament or vary the rhythm, as in the piece at the top in the picture. Larger beads can also be included. Make the clasp as shown in the drawing above.

FLOWERS

FLOWERS 1

Are you looking for a very light, filigree strand that is very attractive and yet really simple to make? All you need is ten gilded double spirals and sixty little flowers. And here's how you make it: Cut the double spirals apart with your pliers and slide three flowers onto each of the spirals, which now number twenty. Thanks to the tight curves, they will stay in place all by themselves—two will always look up, and if you put the third one on the other way round, it will look down. Onto the ends of the spirals, you will slide delicate gilded end pieces, such as those used for stick pins. The spirals can be bound with the help of small rings, which always take one or two windings. Now add a closing, and you are finished: a simple and at the same time refined strand that has every chance of becoming one of your favorite pieces.

FLOWERS 2

For this necklace you should select a particularly nicely structured heavy link chain with a matte surface. In case you need to shorten the chain, individual links can be opened relatively easily at the seam by using two pairs of pliers. Lay out a suitable piece and tie two 50 cm long PVC bands (1.2 mm thick) to the farthest link. On the first band, thread two or three of the small blossoms before you run it through the next link and again thread on a few flowers (see the drawing). When you have reached the other end, knot the PVC band temporarily and work the second band on the opposite sides of the chain links. When all the flowers are in place—it looks especially nice if you put a few gilded flowers among the pastel colors—loosen the temporary knots on both sides and put on a push-snap fastener clasp (see the drawing). The chain is finished with a swivel hook or a twist clasp.

FLOWERS 3

Out of more than 200 small blossoms in delicate pastel shades, you can conjure up this beautiful garland of flowers. For it, you need two curled nylon filaments, 50 to 60 cm long (for the curling technique, see page 12). With the help of a press-molded bead, form a small eyelet at one end of each. Now you can thread on groups of flowers and small gold elements in a casual succession. When the strand has attained the desired length and the arrangement pleases you, make another eyelet. So the necklace will fit comfortably around the neck, make the inner strand somewhat shorter and less lavishly filled than the other. For the clasp, see page 14.

FLOWERS 4

Such a luxuriant bunch of grape blossoms, used as an earring, will go together with all the flower necklaces shown, and can be made quickly. For each earring, put about twenty blossoms on a pin and form a small eyelet. With every four flowers, make one of five not overly narrow rings, hang them one inside another, and fasten them to the ear clip with a small ring. For this opulent grape design, you should select a clip that is simple, but not too small, so that the sizes are compatible. The pendant, being rather wide, looks more delicate if you use a small ring to attach a slim element, like the feather on the model, to finish it.

FLOWERS 5

There's no question about it: Wearing such a cloth, you will attract attention. And it is simple to make, even though you need a bit of patience in addition to a needle and thread. Cut a long triangle out of some lacy cloth that should not be overly filigreed. Sew as many flowers as you please onto the firmer areas. It looks especially nice if you mix various pastel shades with a scattering of golden blossoms. Some 500 flowers were sewn to this elegant fabric, but even with less material you can achieve a magical effect.

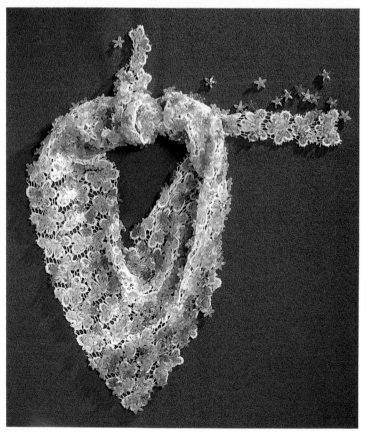

FLOWERS 6

It is true: For this floral corsage you really need a touch of courage, but if you wear it in a festive combination with a matching skirt and blazer, no one is likely to steal the show from you. The most important factor: Sew the flowers really close together, so that they overlap and form a thick carpet that sparkles very magically in the light of evening (some 500 silvery blossoms sparkle on the model!). The admiration you gain will repay you for the laborious work of sewing! An added touch is the big silver snail—originally meant for an earring—at the angle of the decolletage.

FLOWERS 7

This threaded strand features a contrast of summery blue and yellow. Thread on whatever beads you have or choose, and put on a big daisy for added emphasis. A little trick holds the flower in position and prevents it from turning: thread on a flower petal facing the front, then a thin metal tube and, if necessary, another bead—both elements being behind the flower—and then draw the thread from back to front at the opposite petal. If you like, you can heighten the effect of the strand by attaching a second daisy to an overbutton (see page 10) and thus decorating a blouse button.

FLOWERS 8

Four eye-catching daisy blossoms turn this extraordinary summer strand into something remarkable. The basis is a transparent PVC band about 60 cm long, with a diameter of 5 mm, and some 10-12 meters of a soft and easily bent wire which is given a soft shimmery look by a transparent nylon coating. Cut off about two meters of the thin wire and bend it loosely around the PVC band. Here your work does not have to be very precise. When you have bent about 40 cm, slide the spiral off the carrier band and put it aside for the time being. In a second step, wrap the PVC band, the length of which you have determined in advance, very carefully with the thin wire. You can make the beginning easier by attaching the wrapping wire firmly to the PVC band with a small piece of wire. Try it and see which wrapping technique is easiest for you. Sometimes it goes especially well if you twist the PVC band while you let the thin wire slide through between the thumb and index finger of your other hand. In any case, make sure that you wrap the spirals tightly and evenly.

Before you install the push snap fastener permanently, slide one end of the loose spiral you have already pre-pared into it, and drape the wire around the band with a touch of imagination.

Two of the enameled daisy blossoms are attached directly to the strand, while the other two hang from small rings. Experiment a bit to find out which position looks especially natural and harmonious.

EYE-CATCHERS

EYE-CATCHER 1

Can such a thing be a necklace? Yes, of course it can, if you want it to! The trick is the delicate link chain of white plated material and tiny gold clamps. Cut seven strands, each about 1.20 meters long, and remove the last plate very carefully with pliers. With a steady hand, you can slide a thin nylon filament, onto which you will thread the large beads (double the filament), into the small linking ring. Hold them in place with a press-molded bead, and thread one small pearl onto each filament, which is now single again, and close each with another press-molded bead. To lighten the mood, thread several large and small beads between the links of the chain. You can wear this piece open—no fear, the big beads provide weight and nothing can slide—or make a knot of all the strands (Caution: the strands can get tangled easily!).

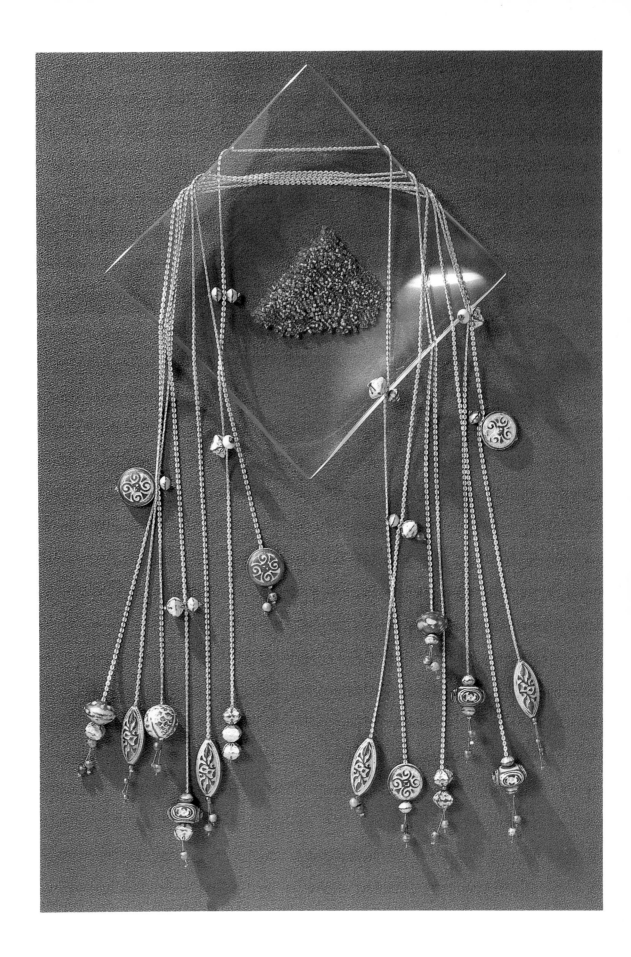

EYE-CATCHER 2

Sphere, cone, and cord, harmonizing in color and size and quickly combined to make the pendant on the left in the picture. It is easy to make: Slide a PVC band (1.2 mm thick) 20 cm long through the eyelet of the cone and the big bead, and tie the band to the cord. Onto each end thread two beads of suitable colors, and attach them with knots. To make it look more fancy, tie another short PVC band on and thread a few nice beads onto it. A cord clasp is used in an odd way for the strand on the right: Join two pieces of cord (25 and 18 cm long) with gilded cord catches. The actual clasp is the one at the right; the eyelets on the left were linked by a ring. A third clasp eyelet holds the actual pendant, which is closed by a short metal tube. Tie pieces of a PVC band (1.2 mm thick, about 10 cm long) to this short piece of cord, and slide decorative elements that please you and blend with the cord in terms of color and style onto the ends. For this model, glittering gold balls with transparent beads and striking chased pearl buttons were combined. Make sure that you pull the band tight and push the closing knot as near the beads as possible, so the elements stay firmly in place. The knot will hold very well, and you can trim off the excess. The gilded hat gives the pendant a particular elan. It is attached directly to the cord with a rhinestone pin.

EYE-CATCHER 3

What looks at first glance to have been cast is put together with a few knots. And so it goes, step by step: Use a piece of nylon filament (about 15 cm long) to make a loop around a transparent PVC band (5 mm thick) long enough to fit around your neck. Put the ends together and thread the large elements and the small closing bead on, securing them with a press-molded bead. Pull it tight enough so the upper loop cannot slide any more. Step two: For the "side piece" on the left, double a piece of nylon filament about 15 cm long and thread the two ends together through a curved tube and a large disc. Secure them with a press-molded bead and trim off the excess. Tie a PVC band onto the main strand, thread the "side piece" on and make a second knot. Onto the end pieces—this is the last step—tie two big beads. If you want, you can add two smaller beads with another piece of PVC band, and the main job is done! Now all you need will be two side tubes and a suitable clasp.

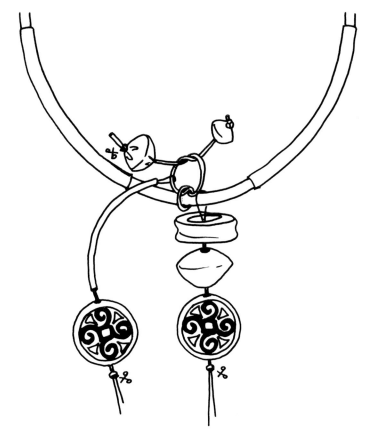

EYE-CATCHER 4

Such an earring really looks unique alone. And how is it made? As follows: Through the last links of three chains of varying lengths, slide a small piece of nylon filament and thread both ends through a flat disc bead. Put on a press-molded bead and trim off the excess. Now slide a short nylon filament through the bottom link of each chain, double the ends, and thread the large and small beads on. A press-molded bead holds the arrangement in place (and a smaller bead prevents the press-molded bead from sliding into the hole of the large bead). Now thread one or two small beads on each and add another press-molded bead some distance from the end. It will look nice if a bit of the nylon filament remains visible. The earring is held on by a clip that you can glue onto the back of the upper disc.

EYE-CATCHER 5

The mystery of what the material of this unusual necklace is cannot be solved easily. It is very durable aqua-leather, which is made from fish skin (see "Materials") and is easy to work. Coat a carrier cord, about 50 cm long, with quick-drying glue and press an already cut piece of leather firmly onto it (be sure to keep the seam in the right location!). Now cut it to the right length, glue the end caps on, and attach a clasp. Wrap a diagonally cut piece of leather around the middle and pull both ends through a not overly narrow oval ceramic ring. Trim off the leather piece until the whole thing looks good to you. A few glued-on rhinestones provide sparkling accents.

CONTRASTS

CONTRAST 1

A strong contrast looks lively. Be
brave and make unusual combinations
with strong colors and impressive beads!

CONTRAST 2

Silver is a mitigating measure in strong black-and-white contrasts, and thus austere nobility characterizes these two threaded strands. The model on the left is made with two nylon filaments each one meter long; the pair of tubes will be put on separately and fixed parallel to each other by separating elements on either side. With experience in threading, your eye will be trained to see an entire composition, but it is best to check your arrangement again and again in the mirror.

The beautiful glass plates on the right come from Murano, are hand-made, and a genuine silver inlay makes them glitter. Such extraordinary elements make their best impression in a simple environment, as here, where smooth silver tubes were selected.

The element with the double tubes is held by the small pendant. You can work it from bottom to top with a doubled PVC band.

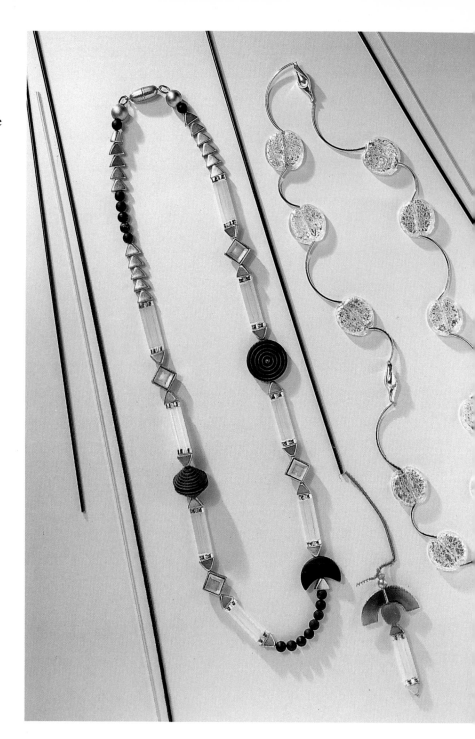

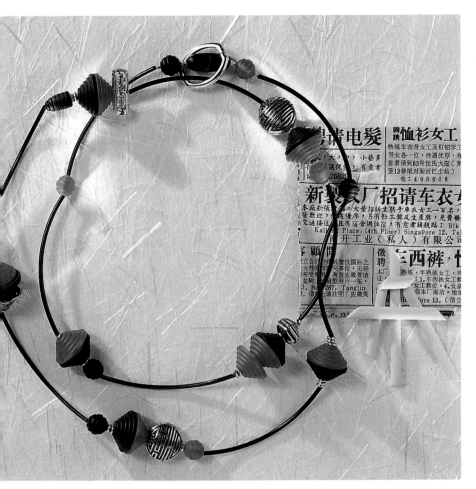

CONTRAST 3

This will appear Chinese to you: A black dress, a gray Rolli and a necklace in Chinese style! Mix whatever you like, heartily and pleasingly: black tubes with red and black grooved cones, plus Chinese ornaments in glittering gold. If you make the strand without a clasp, you can add a snap clasp later and wear it short.

CONTRAST 4

These Chinese-flavored earrings are made by mixing elements. The black tassel, which can be had in the Parament trade, turns the earring on the right, which is worked from top to bottom, into a remarkably eye-catching piece of jewelry. Onto the middle of a nylon filament about 15 cm long, slide a piece of aluminum tubing 4 cm long and form a loop. Pass the two ends of the fila-ment, which should be the same length, through the gold cap, the two grooved conical beads, a small golden bead and the closing cap. Finally, attach the decorative tassel and the round Chinese disc, secure your composition with a press-molded bead, and hang the loop on a half-creole clip.

For the earring at the left, which is worked from bottom to top, take the first step by attaching a small ring to each eyelet of the gilded staff. The two lower rings hold the Chinese disc, and the upper two are joined by a third ring. Pass a piece of nylon filament about 10 cm long through this ring and then push both ends through the gold cap and the grooved conical beads. A small ring unites the impressive earring with a clip.

CONTRAST 5

An exotic breath of the Far East becomes tangible in this effective contrast of satiated red with deep black. For the necklace on the left, work a clasp onto a black cord about 90 cm long. A nice thick tassel—a very important accessory for a piece of jewelry in a Chinese style—can be found in the trade with a little luck. Draw a 15 cm nylon filament through the eyelet of the tassel and with the two ends put together, thread the black half-moon, the small red bead, and finally the cord onto it. Make sure to pull the cord through to the middle of it. A small additional tube can be very helpful, if the nylon filament is not firm enough (see page 12). To finish it, thread on a small metal hat, crowned by a small round bead. Put on a press-molded bead and pull hard on the nylon. Trim off the excess. And now, to finish the job, add the main accent: a round red grooved disc, which you glue to the lower half of the black half-moon. If the proportions are right and the red is the right shade, it looks very attractive—and very Chinese!

The shapes of the golden beads and the big milk-white ring of the necklace on the right are very harmoniously suited to each other, and it is easy to associate a Chinese lantern with this pendant. Here too, begin with the tassel, through the eyelet of which you thread a nylon filament. All the other elements are, as before, threaded on with the two ends together. A press-molded bead forms the closing.

CONTRAST 6

The noble contrast of black and white, accented by a slight addition of gold, should be accentuated by a striking leather band—in the model, a band of fish leather. Cut the leather band to about 75 cm and attach a push-snap fastener clasp and swivel hook. Put beads and cones of your choice onto a stick pin, and penetrate the front of the leather band with it. Only as much of the pin should remain visible as you need to apply the end piece. For safety's sake, put a drop of glue on the pin, so the clasp won't come loose. The strand that lies across it is threaded. Select black and white beads whose diameters are suited to the openings of the black spirals. Add a clasp of your choice.

CONTRAST 7

This clever pendant on a leather band really makes a red T-shirt come alive. The dreamy little grape is threaded on: slide about 25 tiny black and the same number of white beads onto short pins, and add a small glass rod to about one-third of them, so that the pins can be arranged more pleasantly. Now slide the prepared pins onto a black leather band, bring the ends together, and thread six black end caps and one ceramic piece on. When you like the composition—you have to move the individual parts around a bit until they are in the right place—then knot the leather band. Before you pull the knots tight, though, push a second leather band through. To finish the job, determine the final length and attach push snap fastener clasps and a twist clasp.

What would the earring on the left be without the lively red bead! Its inner nature consists of an extended spiral, to which you add alternating black and white beads and finally a colorful, especially eye-catching single piece. The chief difficulty is that of bending the two ends of the very inflexible spiral together. But with a lot of feeling, you will succeed in bending the straight end, onto which you have threaded the beads, into an eyelet and attaching it to the other end of the spiral. Find out where a small ring is best attached, and attach a simple clip to it.

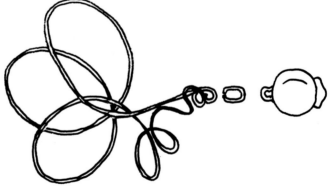

CONTRAST 8

A long pin links these two wonderfully contrasting beads made of Murano glass. Begin with the square bead, then put on the smaller round bead and insert the pin into the transverse hole from the bottom, then to the side, and back out one of the two lower holes. Attach the triangular bead as close to the tube as possible, pull the filament tight again, and bend the excess of the pin into a small eyelet. To make the neck ring, draw three nylon filaments, each about 45 cm long, through the upper hole in the silver tube and thread beads and long thin tubes on according to either the picture or your own preference. So that the three strands will not push against each other too much, push several beads with a large interior diameter over all three strands. When the neck ring has the correct length, bend the strands together to form an eyelet, put on a large press-molded bead that you finish off with a large-holed bead, and attach a simple swivel hook as a clasp.

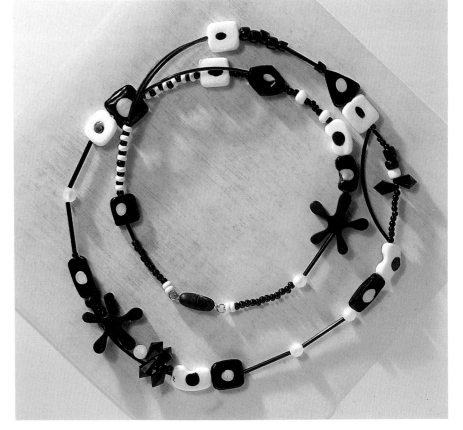

CONTRAST 9

The mixture makes this threaded strand come alive, and when making it, you should let yourself be guided completely by the optical impression. If the first attempt does not please you, simply try it a second time. Make the strand on two nylon filaments, so you can form individual sections parallel to each other, which will make for a light and refined effect. For the model, a twist clasp was installed, but if the necklace is long enough, you can do without a clasp altogether.

FESTIVE AND EXTRAVAGANT

FESTIVE AND EXTRAVAGANT 1

The character of these lavish necklaces is yours to define through your
choice of decorative elements. A dark
slate-gray color and the shimmer of
gold-plated beads in an extravagant
variety of shapes give the model a
weighty, powerful air. A piece of jewelry
for the evening, it unfolds its entire
charm only in romantic soft light. It is
made in a similar way to the Africa 4
model but has a very different character.
Choose a transparent PVC band of 5 mm
diameter as the carrier, and a likewise
transparent PVC band, 1.2 mm thick, to
attach to it. Attach pieces 20 to 25 cm
long to the carrier band, thread the
individual pieces onto them, and secure
them with simple knots. The thinner
band can be knotted firmly and permanently with a relatively strong pull. But
make sure to put on a small bead in
front of elements with a wide hole, to
prevent the knot from pulling through.
The necklace should be particularly
lavish in the middle and simpler to the
sides. It is best to check the way the
elements lie again and again. When you
like what you see and the strand has
become lavish enough, push curved
tubes on and add a clasp (see page 14).

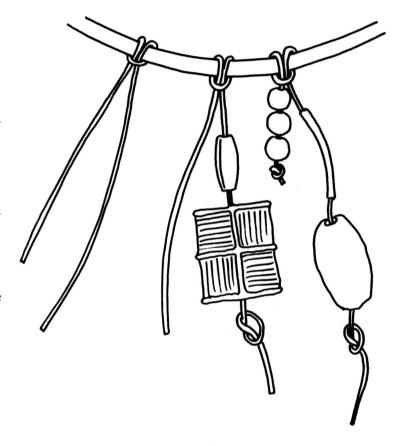

What a glow from 140 gilded beads! You need a natural-colored leather band of 3 to 3.5 mm thickness, 70 thin leather bands with a length of 20 cm each, and a pair of pliers. First determine the overall length of the strand, and then attach the thin leather bands to the main strand as the drawing shows. Pull the loops tight, but make sure that they remain moveable.

Now slide the gilded beads onto the thin bands and secure them by knotting the leather bands. Some bands should be a little longer than others, so that the beads can be pushed close together. Use the pliers to pull the leather band tight, but be careful: An overly strong pull can cause the band to break. When all the pearls are knotted in place, arrange them a bit, thread two tubes on in the back, and fasten on a push-snap fastener clasp. One more tip: The strand takes on a very different character when colored beads are used instead of the gilded elements, and perhaps a different-colored leather band should be selected. Just give it a try!

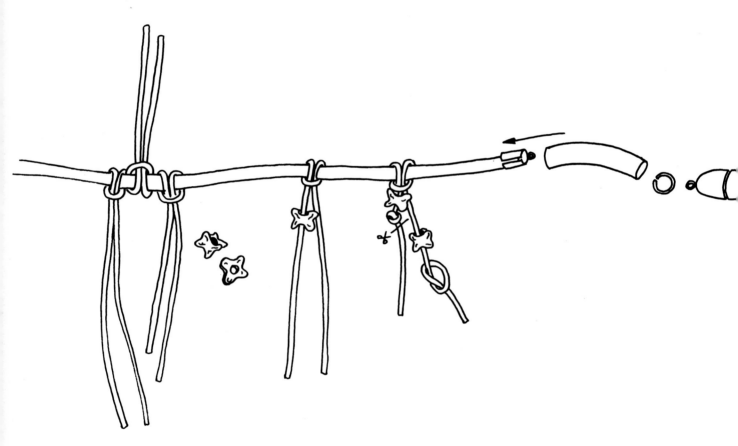

Are you looking for a really striking and glittering piece of jewelry for a very special evening? Then make this necklace, which demands a lot of time and material but will surely win you admiring glances. You make it in two parts, and for the first step you need 78 small metal tubes about 1.8 cm long and three meters of transparent PVC band (1.2 mm thick). Slide three tubes onto the center of the band and form a triangle with them. The knot has to be pulled tight and pushed right up against the tubes. Form a second triangle by threading two tubes onto one band and just one onto a second, and tie them again. Make all 26 triangles in the same way. Be careful to put two tubes on the longer band and only one on the shorter one so as to use the total length. To close the band, knot it several times and trim off the excess. Don't let it bother you if the triangle strand does not look too orderly and even.

For the second part you need 100 to 120 drops of plastic (glass would be too heavy), the same number of gold beads and pins, plus 60 cm of PVC band. Onto every pin, place a bead and a drop, and secure them with a small eyelet. Once this tedious work is behind you, unite the drops and the triangles by running the line through one triangle, threading on three or four drops, and drawing the band through the next triangle. At first the strand will surely look a bit bulky and shapeless, but when you have added on all the drops, put the necklace on, and it will take on its final lavish appearance. To attain the desired length, thread on a few large gold beads at each end and install a push snap fastener. Now you need only the appropriate dress and the right occasion to show off this bewitching necklace.

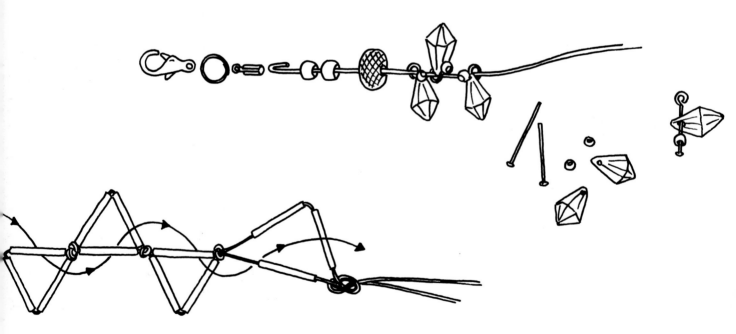

For this shimmering necklace you
need beads in four different sizes, and a
lot of time and patience to attach them.
Instead of the low-priced wax beads,
that flake off easily and aren't worth the
trouble, select real glass beads, which
are far more durable. Set some 75 to 80
beads of two different sizes on 3.5 cm
long eyelet pins, shorten the excess if
necessary, and make an eyelet at the far
end with pliers. Put five of the smallest
beads on straight or eyelet pins, bend
the remainder into a small eyelet, and
hang them on the big beads (see the
drawing). When you have finished all
your strings in this manner—you will
find that, with growing experience,
pinning gets easier and easier!—then
thread them alternately with single
beads onto a nylon filament about 50 cm
long. Leave out the intermediate single
pearls in the central area, and the
necklace will look particularly lavish!
Now determine the final length and put
on a push snap fastener. For such a
costly and festive necklace, you should
select a nice screw clasp to add to the
elegance.

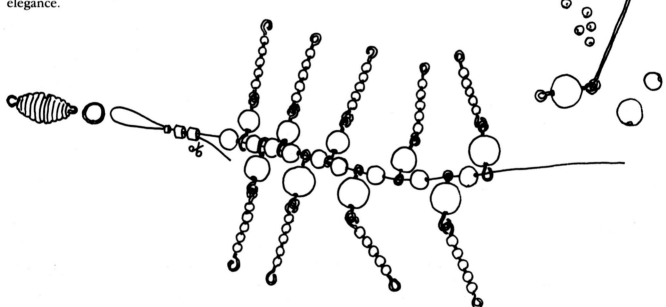

It is often very astonishing what an impressive effect can be achieved with what small means. For example, take this strand made of many small beads, with their matte shimmer and their harmonious colors. You need about 160 small beads and a few larger ones of suitable colors per strand, and for every color, a nylon filament some 60-70 cm long. Before you begin to thread the beads, curl the filament the way you do with gift-wrapping cord, by pulling it over pliers (see page 12). But be careful: If you pull too hard, the filament will break.

Thread the bigger beads at irregular intervals among the small ones. Once you have finished all the strands and determined the length of the necklace, make a small eyelet at each end of each strand with the help of a press-molded bead. Thread the eyelets on one end of each strand onto a small piece of PVC band 1.2 mm thick, likewise the other ends, and thread each end through a metal cap. Apply the clasp as shown in the drawing.

If you want the necklace to be livened up by an additional focal point, make up about six decorative elements, each consisting of two metal tubes about 3 cm long (3 mm diameter), and two times two beads, which you thread onto a piece of PVC band 15 cm long. Tie the band tightly and hide the knot in one of the tubes. The six tube elements can be pushed over the ends of the strands of beads, draped decoratively—and now you have one more extraordinary piece of jewelry.

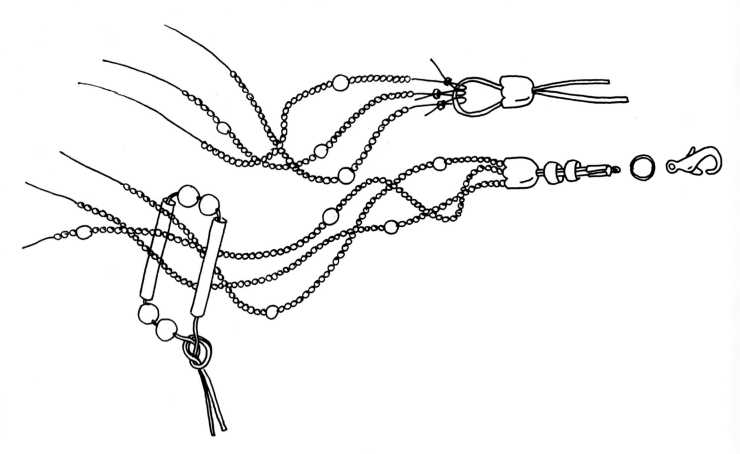

The mixture of shimmering white beads and glittering gold gives every piece of jewelry a delicate and elegant tone. This is exactly right for a formal necklace that, despite its simplicity, requires the touch of nimble fingers. It is above all else the staffs of beads that create the effect, but they also require the most work. First thread about 200 cream-colored rocaille beads onto a golden wire about 0.4 mm thick. With a small piece of wire, fasten the gold wire to a PVC band (transparent, about 8 cm long and 5 mm thick), that you now wrap with the beaded wire. This is not simple, and you can make the work easier by holding the end of the wire with your lips and turning only the PVC band. Just try it! Attach the end of the thin strand of beads with a piece of wire and leave about half a centimeter free, just as at the beginning. Onto each end slide a small metal cap with an eyelet, after having put a drop of glue into the cap. Push it on tightly—and it's finished!

The gold-colored tubes and some especially striking beads form the three sections of the strand between the bead staffs. For each section, thread a piece of nylon filament through the eyelet of a staff and run the ends of the nylon either separately through two thin metal tubes or together through the larger decorative elements. The link to the next staff is formed with a press-molded bead. Small rings link the individual elements of this lovely strand, which can be made without a clasp.

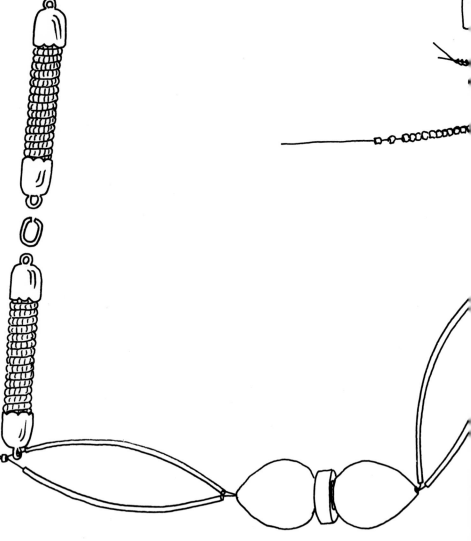

You make this strand in individual
sections with PVC bands 15 to 20 cm
long (1.2 mm thick). Two types of
changeable, slightly flattened beads
make a nice contrast with the highly
polished gold tubes. Thread two beads
onto a PVC band, a tube onto each side,
followed by another bead. Then tie a
knot and pull it very tight, so that the
individual ring is under tension. Place
the knot between two beads and trim off
the excess. A really tight knot will
disappear into the hole of a bead and
will not open. Pull the next band
through between two beads and make it
the same way. When the strand has
reached the desired length, draw a last
piece of band through two beads, then
pull both ends of it through a single
bead and secure it with a push snap
fastener. The second strand is made in
the same way and hung on the split ring
of the first strand. For the model, a
simple swivel hook was chosen, but
naturally, a decorative twist catch could
also be used.

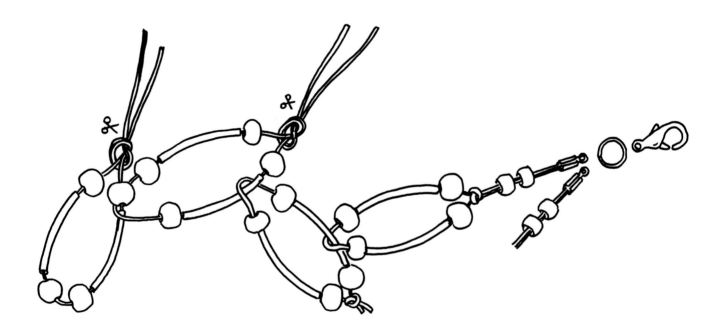

...ft strand:

... simple pullover is the ideal
...er for this strand, which is as
...ve as it is easy to make. The
...tial part is the link chain, open at
...ottom, to which you attach the sun
...oon with small rings. The chain is
...ogether by a flat snail, which you
...ttach with small rings. Make the
... a little bit asymmetrical, so it will
...especially striking and exciting—if
...ks unusual, it is right!

Right strand:

This eye-catching piece can be made
in no time. For it, you need about 45
cm of black PVC band, 5 mm thick, onto
which you slide two curved tubes with
an appropriate diameter and a particularly attractive central piece, here an
unusually large gilded ceramic element.
The closing is formed by two push-snap
fastener clasps of 5 mm diameter, to
which you attach a swivel hook and
several split rings, which allow you to
change the length of this close-fitting
necklace slightly.

...vo simple strands that you can
... very easily: Separate intermediate
...s interrupt the quiet flow of the
...hain on the left, which is about 50
...ng and was made without a clasp.
... the intervals at which you add the
...ative elements completely up to
... magination. Make sure that the
...hook fast, but without any projec-
...that might make the piece of
...ry catch on your clothing.

The cross hangs on two leather
bands that are held together by gilded
beads with large holes and knotted in
rustic fashion. Wrap a piece of natural
leather band, 1 mm thick, around the
cross as additional decoration, and knot
it in the back. The pendant receives its
final touch from gilded miniature
elements that are hung on with small
rings.

These two necklaces reward the work of rather laborious preparation with simple elegance and a touch of refinement. The shimmering shell bears its secrets on its reverse side: a metal part with two thin tubes (see drawing). This added part can also be obtained singly and can be glued very simply to the back of flat fashion jewelry components (see the "Refinement" section). Slide a piece of silver wire about 15 cm long and 1 mm thick through the metal tubes of the snail, making a U shape, and out again through the left and right holes in the glittering metal tube. Pull both ends tight and make sure that the metal tube and the snail shell are firmly attached to each other. Cap the silver wire about 1 cm back and roll the ends with your bead pliers into a decorative spiral of two or three coils. When the metal tube is firmly in place, slide the pendant onto a simple necklace and you're finished!

The golden necklace on the right requires somewhat more nimble fingers and develops the possibilities of the little metal tube further. In the first step, slide a pin, 6 cm long, through the hole in the flat black disc and, from inside, back out through one of the first two lateral holes in the glittering little tube. Now put a suitable bead on it, pull the pin tight, shorten it to 0.5 cm and use the bead pliers to make a small eyelet in it. Ha[...] spiral of gold wire, which you pull a[...] forms a loose contrast and finishes o[...] the lower hole in the opposite side. Slide the long end of the spiral into [...] small hole from outside, upward and [...] of the tube, and then in again from outside. The tension of the spiral ho[...] it in place. Now thread a nylon filam[...] some 50 cm long through the upper [...] holes in the metal tube, and add a be[...] a big neck ring and six more beads o[...] each side. Before you secure all of th[...] with a press-molded bead, check the [...] seat of all the elements, which shoul[...] have only a little bit of play. A screw [...] finishes the job.

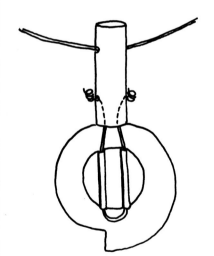
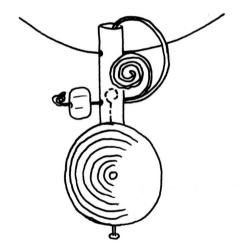
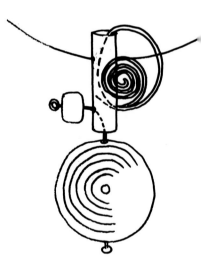

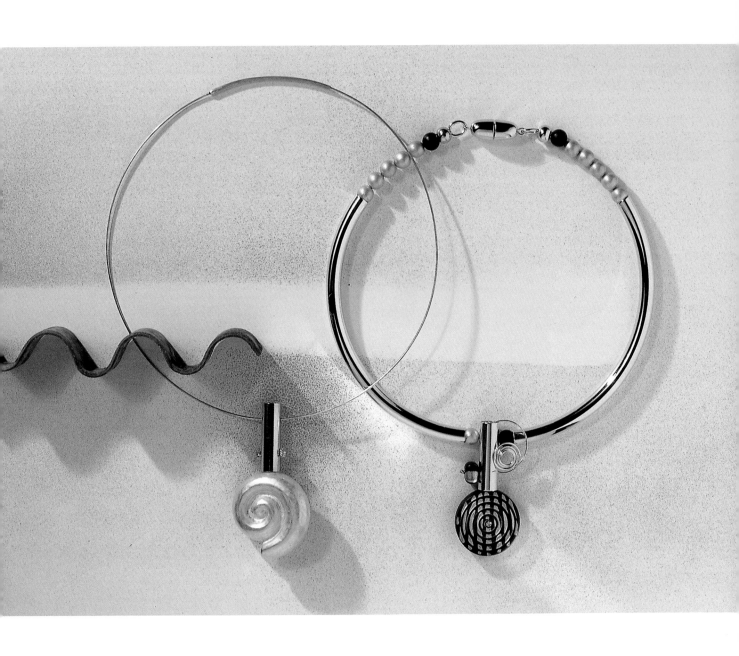

The contrast between deep black and glittering gold really looks noble, doesn't it? The pendant on the left is made in two steps. First cut a piece of PVC band about 50 cm long and 1.2 mm thick and thread on six of the black rods, which actually belong to a clasp and are used here simply for decoration. Attach the two ends of the band together and thread them through a large flat ceramic piece, a not too small bead, and a thin metal tube about 3 cm long. Put this component aside for a moment and make the second element directly on the cord. To do this, slide a black bead, a gold cap and the second ceramic piece onto a pin and make an eyelet. The arch of the gold cap should surround the bead. Take the element you made first and thread the open ends of the PVC band through the eyelet of the pin. For the final step, knot the ends of the band several times, and very tightly, to the black cord, arrange the two ceramic discs, and determine the length of the entire strand, which will be closed by a cord clasp.

The charm of the short strand in the middle is embodied in its cord that hangs down loosely. It is made of three pieces of black cord, about 50, 30 and 20 cm long, which you will cut and secure at both ends with transparent tape. Then fit three black pearls, each with a gold cap, onto pins as a decorative element and add one ceramic disc each to two of the three pins. The strand has a more exciting effect if you select discs of different sizes. Now secure the pins with small eyelets and fasten the two ceramic discs, slightly overlapping, to the longest of the three prepared pieces of cord with a short piece of PVC band. Attach each end of this strand to one end of the two shorter pieces and hold them fast with tape. Put a little glue into two metal caps and press the cord in. The shorter piece of cord ends behind the smaller disc, where it is held by a piece of wire; the longer piece is attached to the main strand twice behind the longer strand, and the end is allowed to hang down (see the drawing). Push the firmly

attached end into a metal cap. A small bead cap decorates the end, and a few hooks and eyes complete the necklace.

For the strand on the right, fit a cord of the desired length with a cord clasp, and glue the ends of a short piece into two gilded caps. Secure one end a nylon filament about 10 cm long with a press-molded bead and thread on a small bead, a black glass rod, and over another bead of Murano glass (the glass rod remains visible in the inside of the bead). Then come four already prepared gold caps with beads inside (pinned) and the prepared short piece of cord. Penetrating the cords can be done very easily if you pull the wire through a small auxiliary tube, which you have already inserted into the cord and then removed (see the "Techniques" chapter). Push the wire through the main strand of the cord in this manner as well, and put on two press-molded beads. They can be pushed into a cord very easily. Two additional beads close off and cover up the seam.

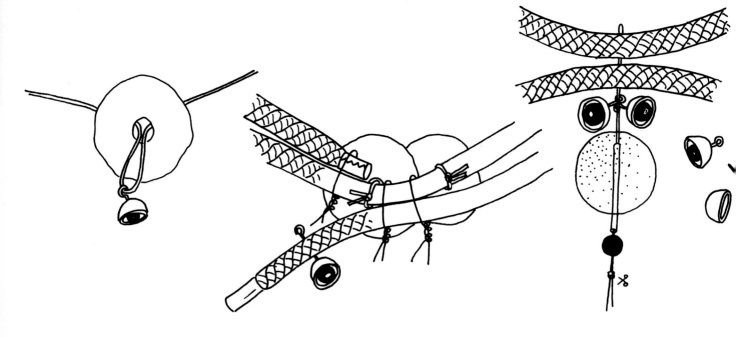

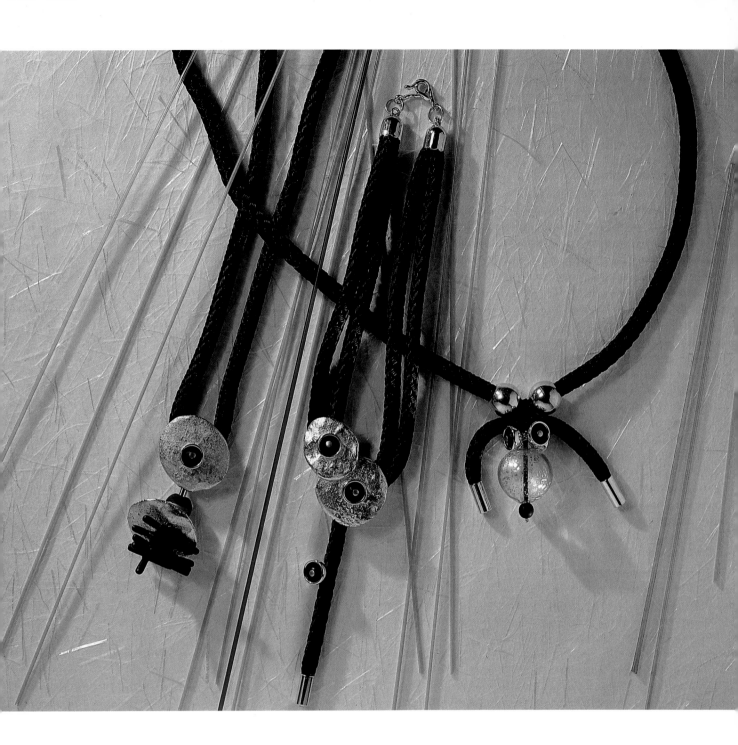

This strong and striking strand is made in three parts. First make the right side strand by tying three cotton bands, about one meter long, firmly together at one end. To do this, you can use either transparent tape or wire. Twist one of the three bands about nine times around the other two bands and slide three ornamental rings with big holes over all three strands to secure and decorate them. Wrap one of the two remaining bands around the other two in the same manner, again slide two ornamental rings on, and repeat the wrapping process one last time with the third long band. Be sure to wrap as evenly, firmly, and without gaps as

possible. When you have finished the desired length, secure the ends with a small piece of wire wrapped tightly around all three bands. Onto each remaining piece, thread a small metal disc; then knot the three bands at different lengths. Make the second side the mirror image of the first and secure the three bands with a few twists of wire before you unite the two parts, also with wire.

The basis of the very lavish piece in the center is a so-called "net" of metal, through the small holes of which you thread a piece of wire about 50 cm long to attach small decorative elements—in the model, they are leaves and pieces of

hematite (see the drawing). Even if it may look a little strange at the beginning, the more lavish you make it, the more effective the pendant will be. It is important that you pull the thin wire very tight, but if it should remain too loose, you can use pliers to pull it a little bit more from the back. You can fasten the finished net to the front and center of the necklace with wire and conceal the joint of the two strands. To finish the job, select metal caps that will cover the glue points of the beginning, or, as on the model, two push snap fasteners. The necklace is closed by a swivel hook and several split rings.

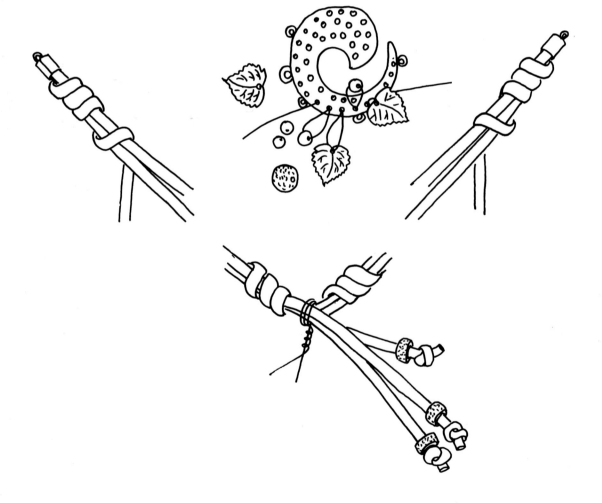

FESTIVE AND
EXTRAVAGANT 13

No one can tell by looking at this piece of jewelry that you made it at the last minute. Everything that you need for the short strand on the left is certainly to be found in your supplies: several striking beads—here they are costly individual pieces plated with real gold or silver—thin metal tubes, and a few small beads. Bring two pieces of nylon filament together around back, but separate them in front with beads and tubes, and close the strand with a twist clasp or swivel hook.

For the strand on the right, place a few pieces that harmonize in color and style on a pin, penetrate the thick cord, and put on the clasp. If you like, you can add another accent with a small rhinestone pin.

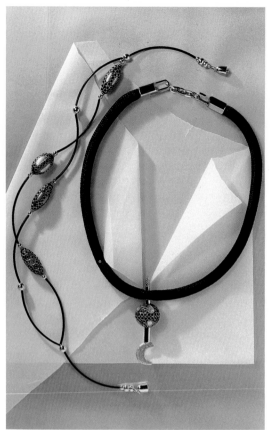

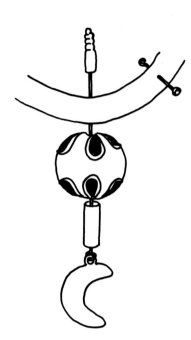

FESTIVE AND
EXTRAVAGANT 14

This is a strikingly decorated necklace, which you begin to make by sliding one large bead over each of two thin, curved silver tubes. They should stay firmly in place so as not to shift while the necklace is being worn. Thread the tubes, along with the beads, onto long pins, form a small eyelet, and tie them separately to the middle of the thicker PVC band with transparent PVC bands. To make the strand look a little more lavish, knot a third band. Slide beads of various shapes and sizes onto the six band ends and tie the band so it will be very stiff and short. The transparent square bead will reflect the light very nicely, and the silver moon can be attached by its small eyelet.

he six-sided beads take on even
 glitter when they are not
ded, but pinned. For the strand on
:ft, you need about 400 beads in
or three harmonizing colors—a test
ur dexterity and patience when it
:s to pinning them. In the second
 you make the pendant with the big
, which you see, slightly varied, on
ecklace on the right. For it, make a

tiny eyelet (using a press-molded bead)
on a nylon filament about 20 cm long,
and then thread on some 25 of the
pinned beads. Then come the other
elements, including the long golden
tube, and you finish it off with a six-
sided bead and a press-molded bead.

When you select the materials, make
sure that the opening in the big bead is
wide enough to take the tip of the

tapered tube. Slide the pendant onto
the transparent PVC band, which is
about 60 cm long and 1.2 mm thick, and
thread on the pinned beads, casually
mixed as to colors, on both sides.
Intersperse gilded six-sided beads at
regular intervals to give the strand a
lighter atmosphere and add their typical
glitter. Find a simple twist clasp for this
heavy strand.

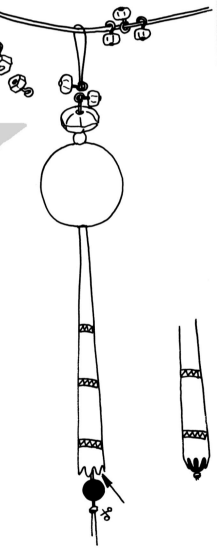

These three pinned strands can be made quickly and add the ideal touch to your favorite blouses. From the plentitude of colors and shapes, choose the prettiest and begin to work. Select pins of various lengths and bend them to make a small eyelet at one end before you put on the elements as your imagination suggests. Be brave; whatever pleases you is allowed, and a colorful mixture of beads in different sizes and small metal parts will create a very lively effect. Leave a piece of the metal pin free at the endw so you can bend it into an eyelet. Before you close the eyelet completely, attach the next pin.

LOTS OF BEADS

Glass and ceramic beads offer your imagination a lot of scope. But that is another subject—for another book.